SNAPSHOTS OF LIFE
from a Writer's View

Carol Goodman Heizer

Copyright © 2014 by Carol Goodman Heizer, M.Ed.
All rights reserved. Published by Alpha Publishing,
Division of Alpha Consulting, 2014,
with permission of the author.

Except for brief quotations and excerpts as permitted
under the United States Copyright Act of 1976,
no part of this publication may be reproduced in
print or electronic, without written permission of
the author or publisher.

ISBN: 0-978-1-929251-04-9
Additional copies available on-line at:
amazon.com   or
createspace.com/4786910

Proudly printed and bound in the United States
of America.

Cover photo and all internal photography
copyright ©2014 by Carol Goodman Heizer.
All rights reserved.
Cover design by:
Carol Goodman Heizer, with
Mary Dow Bibb Smith

Dedicated to

To all the world's writers who have been blessed with the ability transform thoughts, visual images, and life's experiences into words on the printed page so that others may broaden their own experiences.

TO:

All of today's writers —

All of those who have gone before us —

And all of those who will follow us!

Acknowledgements

This project would not have been possible without the assistance of several people. I would like to thank the following:

Sarah Heizer, my daughter, who bailed me out of many electronic glitches with her computer expertise.

Linda Cessna, RN, my faithful friend, for her valuable content suggestions and proof-reading ability.

Mary Dow Smith of Home Crafted Artistry and Printing, for formatting and design.

Jake and Rosie, my two four-legged "children," for their ability to make me laugh with their antics when I desperately needed it.

TABLE OF CONTENTS

Introduction: On the Wings of Words i

FAMILY and FRIENDS 1
To You, My Precious Child 3
A Little Boy 4
Little Rubber Ducks 6
Those Old Faded Jeans 7
A Little Girl 8
She's a Teacher Now 10
Grandma's Eyeglasses 12
Climbing the Family Tree 14
Letter to My Ancestors 16
My Great-Grandfather Jacob Frederick Deschler . . 18
Ma and Pa Kesselring: A Trip Down Memory Lane . . 20
Cousin George Armstrong Custer 22
Laquita Enters through an "Open Door" . . . 24

NATURE 25
The Rainbow's Charm 27
The Mountains Rise 29
Listen to the Rocks 30
The Quiet Creek 33
The Lonely Tree 35
Life of the Rainforest Rainbow Lorikeet . . . 36

INSPIRATION 39
The Innocence of Childhood 41
A Touch from the Lord 42
Problems or Power 43
Before, Behind, and Within 44
Limitless Protection 45
Sin to Salvation 46
Why, Lord? 47
In the Still of the Night 48
11 Chronicles 7:14 49
Help for Today, Hope for Tomorrow 50
That Old Rugged Cross 51
The Love of God 53
Knowledge and Wisdom 54
I Hadn't Counted the Cost 55
The Grave 56

OUR WORLD 57
An Emotional World in Which We Live . . . 59
On the Deck of the Ship 60
A Quiet Sunday Afternoon 61
The Unexpected Visitors 62
The Election 63

Sunset at Sea	64
The World from the Top of the Alps	65
White Sands and Waving Palms (Roatán, Honduras)	66
A Tribute to Mount Egmont (New Zealand)	67
Conversing with the Tasman Sea (New Zealand)	68
Landing at Ben-Gurion (Tel Aviv, Israel)	69
The Holy City (Jerusalem, Israel)	70
The Garden of Gethsemane (Jerusalem, Israel)	72
The Sea of Galilee (Tiberias, Israel)	74
Leaving My Spiritual Homeland (Netanya, Israel)	75
Fish and Chips (London, England)	76
The City of Lights (Paris, France)	78
My Ancestors' Homeland (Heidelberg, Germany)	80
The Miner (Hartz Mountains, Germany)	82
A Miner's Life	83
The City Divided (Berlin, Germany)	84
A City of Color (Poznan, Poland)	85
The End of the Line (Auschwitz)	86
The Woodcarving Merchant (Wroclaw, Poland)	88
Not What I Expected (Rome, Italy)	89
A City of Beauty at the Foot of the Mountains (Innsbruck, Austria)	90
To Love the Mountain	90
The Great Wall (China)	91
The Continent—and Country of Australia (Sydney, Australia)	93
The Outback (Alice Springs, Australia)	94

WRITING AND SPEAKING — 95

The Gift Within Me	97
Abstract Thoughts and Concrete Paper	98
Writing Is Like Giving Birth	99
Clothes Make the Man	100

MISCELLANEOUS — 101

My Very Best Friend	103
The Accident	104
The Busy Brain	106
This Empty House	107
The Clock on the Wall	108
The Invitation	110
Hop Scotch House	111

IN MEMORY — 117

A Young Man Named Derrick	119
A Grandfather Named James	120
The First Christmas	122

Introduction
On the Wings of Words

Webster defines word as "a speech sound … a brief expression or remark … a letter or group of letters representing a unit of language." While Webster is correct in his denotation of the word, it simply scratches the surface of the true meaning of words, for these one- or more-than-one letter expressions of thought have wings.

Yes, **wings**!

These wings can carry us across the street as we converse with our neighbor about recent happenings in our area of the city. They allow us to verbally fly into recounts of newspaper articles, descriptions of recently-beheld sunsets, or evaluations of recently seen television shows or movies. These wings can then bring us back into our homes as they allow us to explain to our children how much we love them and how we pray for a divinely-protected and fruitful life for them.

These wings can also carry us across the world as we describe the majesty of the Swiss Alps, the quietness of the Rhine River in Germany, or the Dead Sea in Israel. They allow us to create a mental picture for our listener of the difference between true Italian-made pizza and American pizza. They allow us to tell a story of the appearance of the gondolier and the sound of the waves splashing against the buildings in Venice.

These wings can then fly us back home after our travels and permit us to articulate our deep appreciation for our country and all the freedom it provides. They give us the ability to say, "Thank You, Lord, for the experiences I have been blessed to enjoy and for the peoples I have met and the cultures I have had the privilege to experience. Thank You, Lord, for the blessings You have poured out upon this nation. Oh, Lord, may we return to the Biblical principles upon which this country was founded.

"And thank You, Lord, for the wings of words!"

FAMILY AND FRIENDS

To You, My Precious Child

I am beginning to feel your movements,
And I am feeling *life* within me.
But even before I felt your presence,
My heart was filled with love for you.

I wanted you before you were conceived,
And I had joy in the anticipation.
But once I knew you existed,
My world took on a different focus.

I think of your eyes, your hair,
Your heart and spine and arms and legs.
I wonder about your personality,
And the things you will enjoy in life.

The very thought of you speeds my heart,
And I am privileged to carry you.
I wonder if you are boy or girl,
Or if you'll be tall or short.

You won't be like other children,
For you are far more special.
You are mine, and you are Dad's,
And that makes you unique and priceless.

I cannot wait to meet you, my precious child,
And months seem long as you continue to grow.
But everything needs time, and so do you,
So I'll wait and treasure your movements.

I have a special bond with you, little one,
That no one else can share.
Daddy will feel you from without,
But I feel you from within.

I love you more than words can tell,
And excitement grows with passing days.
Even before you existed on this earthly planet,
You always existed in the mind of God!

A Little Boy

He was a little boy just days ago,
Greeting each day with a cheerful smile –
Happy to be alive and up,
Waiting to be lifted from his wooden crib.

He was a little boy just days ago,
Having worms in his hands, and stones in his pockets.
Having brown eyes that shone like gems,
And wearing a smile that lit the world.

    He was a little boy just days ago,
    Sailing leaf boats in the nearby creek –
    Riding a trike that he thought could fly,
    And playing with cars he thought were Vettes.

        He was a little boy just days ago,
        Wanting a pup but having a rabbit –
        Wanting to swim but fearing the water,
        And jumping off rocks like the ol' Duke Boys.

He was a little boy just days ago,
Hating school and paper work –
Despising his numbers and report card days,
Loving his teachers and their tender touch.

But the years have passed and now he stands,
Not a little boy of just days ago –
But a man standing tall in his rightful place,
Taking a stand for what he knows is right.

Do you remember to take time each day with your children, knowing that the years will pass quickly? Are you making memories to talk about in the future?

Little Rubber Ducks

"I love little rubber ducks,
Speckle-bellied pups,
And I love you."

Those words I heard so often
From the lips of my only son Mark.
They made me laugh –
they always did.

My son knew they would,
And he said them often when I was down.
Didn't matter where he was –
Or what I was doing.

I heard the funny words so often
When frustrations and stresses came.
When tensions built –
When I was blue.

My only son is now gone,
My ears cannot hear those silly words.
The memories linger –
My heart often hears …

"I love little rubber ducks,
Speckle-bellied pups,
And I love you."

Do you have a child in your life that
says funny things to make you smile?
Cherish those moments with them, laugh with them
when they say them, and create memories
to store in your heart for the
remainder of your days.

Those Old Faded Jeans

Those old faded jeans my son would wear
Often had holes where he'd rip and tear.
The hems were ragged, the pockets were torn –
How he loved those old jeans so often worn.
I washed and rinsed and often dried,
But I couldn't hide them however I tried.

I wished for the day when they were so long gone;
I'd probably jump and sing a new song.
What I would give to see those old jeans –
My son wearing them in his early teens.

For you see, my son is no longer here –
He's gone from the earth midst many a tear.
To hear the door open I'd gladly rejoice,
To hear once again his deep, deep voice.
I wouldn't mind those old faded jeans
If my son were in them in his later teens.

*Do you have a special article of clothing
belonging to one of your children? If so,
put it away for safe keeping and,
in the years to come, it will bring you
happy times as you think back
over the years with your beloved child.*

A Little Girl

A little girl just days ago,
With corn silk hair and flashing blue eyes –
The fairest of skin and a will of steel,
She carried the sunshine wherever she went.

A little girl just days ago,
With tiny features and a great big heart –
The bravest of spirits and a questioning mind,
She sought adventure wherever she went.

A little girl just days ago,
With long slender fingers and long curly lashes –
The sharpest of wit and a love for life,
She shouldered the burden for a hurting few.

A little girl just days ago,
With a love for animals from rabbits to horses –
The deepest of affection for all living creatures,
She sought the critters wherever she went.

But the years have passed and now she stands,
Not a little girl of just days ago –
But a woman, a teacher, a refuge for kids,
And a loving mom to her own three "girls."

*Does your child seem to have never-ending energy
and a mile-long list of things they want to do each day?
Do their sparkling eyes and winning smile melt your heart
on days you feel that you are carrying the weight of
the world on your shoulders? Treasure those moments,
for the years will fly by, and they will be grown
and gone before you know it.*

She's a Teacher Now

The years have slipped quickly by, although her days have often seemed long. Teaching in today's classroom is vastly different from the days her mother taught. Society is different, along with students, parents, and most all other aspects of American education.

It is no longer a joy to walk into the classroom, knowing the students show respect they have learned at home. Many students come from one-parent homes where the parent works, and the child has become a "latch key kid."

Other students come from homes where physical and emotional neglect or abuse rule most days. As children follow their parents' example, they carry that lack of discipline or violence into the classroom—and the teacher becomes the referee.

Parents of elementary children are often heard to say, "I don't know what to do with them," and children have learned they can control adults by throwing their temper tantrums to get what they want.

She's a teacher now and refuses to bow down and allow her students to control her classroom simply to avoid a conflict. But she is restricted in so many ways as rules are passed down from the local board of education—rules that tell her she cannot touch the child for fear of parental or legal retribution.

If little Johnny breaks away during a scuffle and inflicts his own bruises, the teacher is always responsible—never little Johnny. After all, perhaps he may have had a difficult life and suffers from a poor self-esteem. We could never run the risk of damaging his fragile ego!

So she struggles each year as children seem to grow more unruly and many parents look to the schools to do the job of raising their children. She maintains her classroom discipline, and the majority of her students are well-behaved. They know she means business when she tells them her expectations.

But her job becomes harder each year as society in general, and students in particular, feel more freedom to exercise their right to behave in whatever manner they choose. So she struggles with the decision to stay in the classroom although she is known by her colleagues as a quality teacher and disciplinarian. It's a shame we are losing so many good teachers—they are simply tired of the fight!

As your child matures and enters the workforce,
can you help to ease their working load by doing little
things for them that will bring a smile to their face?
Perhaps a note of encouragement, an unexpected gift
to arrive at their workplace, or providing an evening meal?
Both of you will benefit from the time spent together.
Love between parent and child can cover a multitude
of stressful situations.

Grandma's Eyeglasses

They didn't look expensive.
They weren't especially pretty to look at.
They were old and bent,
And I wonder how she could see anything through them
But they were Grandma's,
And they were always very special …
Perhaps because SHE was very special.

Grandma always wore her eyeglasses;
I never saw her without them.
Grandma used to call them her "cheaters"
    or "winkers."
She said that's what the older folks called them.
Those old bent glasses …
    they seemed to have magical powers.

When Grandma wore them, she could see
    the beauty of the world around her.
She loved the delicacy of newly-sprouted plants,
The glory of blooming flowers,
And the elegance of a setting sun.
She would look toward the western sky,
 With its beauty more elegant than man could
    ever create,
And smile to herself and say,
"A little bit of Heaven peeking through."

When Grandma wore those eyeglasses,
She could see the joy in everyday things.
She was grateful for each day with which she was blessed
And saw it as a gift from above.
She had known many hard times
And often told me there was a difference
Between happiness and joy …
That happiness is often enjoyed only for a season
And is based upon one's circumstances.
But joy, she said, is the deep, inner peace
That only God can give His children …
That steadfast belief that, whatever the circumstances,
He is still God, and He is still in control

When Grandma wore those eyeglasses,
She could recognize the hurts in other people.
She could see their unspoken needs,
And she did all she could to erase their suffering
    or their loneliness.
At times, it was an afternoon visit or a greeting card
With a hand-written message of hope and encouragement.
Oftentimes it was a loaf of home-made bread.
And still other times, it was a full-course meal.
But always her deeds were accompanied
By prayer beside her bed late at night
When she thought no one was awake.

When Grandma wore those eyeglasses,
She could witness the miracle of her grandchildren
Growing through their trying teen years into adulthood.
She could look beyond the messes we made
And look toward the lessons she taught us.
She could look beyond our foolishness
And see our inherent value.

She wore those glasses to read us Scripture,
And shared how God led in areas of her life.
I always listened when she talked,
For I had watched her life and saw its truth.
I carried her lessons into my marriage,
And I learned from her mistakes.
I had faith in Grandma
Because she had faith in God.

But most of all, when Grandma wore those eyeglasses,
She could see beyond any momentary
    frustration with us,
And see her love for us …
    AND OUR LOVE FOR HER.

*Is there something about your grandparent that you find especially meaningful?
Perhaps it is a personal possession, a family heirloom, or a household item
you often associate with them. Talk to them about it, learn about its origin
or its significance to your grandparent.*

Climbing the Family Tree

Many people insist upon the pedigrees of their pets, yet they are ignorant of their own ancestry. While they want to know the bloodlines of their dogs or cats, they seem to either forget or not care about their own blood lines. And what a shame that is! As one begins to climb the family tree, *surprises* (or perhaps *shocks*) await discovery at nearly every branch. They have lain in wait, hoping for that one curious family member to encounter them.

And, oh, the thrill of that encounter! Perhaps it is a name that is special to the climber. Or perhaps a date that holds special significance! And there those surprises are, simply waiting to amaze that unsuspecting climber.

As we think of our world in scientific or medical terms, we tend to think of atoms, molecules, and cells. But we must never forget that although the universe is made up of such things, life is made up of stories and families, and relationships. Muriel Rukeyser once observed that the universe without its families and their stories would simply be a vast void.

As we climb higher into our family tree, we find ourselves surrounded by thoughts of those we cannot see. We try to picture their faces. Did they have a pleasant appearance? Or were their faces etched in deep furrows of stress and hardship? If we are fortunate enough to have a picture of them, do we find ourselves trying to imagine their personality? What were their concerns, their fears, or their sorrows? As we look back over the centuries, do we find ourselves wondering if our ancestors ever thought ahead to what we might look like? As we look at the legacies that have been left for us by our ancestors, are we doing all we can to leave a legacy of which our future family members would be proud?

We talk of going upward in our family tree, but let us not neglect the importance of going downward into our roots.

Would you like to learn about your family ancestry?
Take the time to inquire while
your family members are still living, for
something may happen unexpectedly, and
you will never have the answers you are
then seeking. Do you have family pictures
with no names? Take the time to learn their identities.
You will be glad you did in the years to come.

Letter To My Ancestors

Dear Ancestors,

Oh, how I wish I could talk to all of you! I know your names and some of the dates related to your lives, but I know little else about some of you. As I have begun researching my family tree, I find myself wanting to learn as much about you as I possibly can. The more I learn, the more I WANT to know. And when I am missing a piece of your life's puzzle, I find myself nearly frantic, at times, trying to fit that piece of your life into my knowledge of you.

I wish I could see your faces, know what kinds of things you enjoyed (if you had time to enjoy anything with all the hard work you had to do raising your families). What lessons could you tell me that you learned in life? What insights could you share with me that would help me not to make some of the mistakes I have made?

Part of me wishes you could come back and live in my world for a while,  but maybe that would be too terrifying for you. How would you adjust to speeding cars, turning electricity on and off with the touch of a switch, ringing cell phones, jet planes, space travel, and high-tech computers small enough to fit into your hand?

If you could step into my life today and see me as one of your descendants, would you be pleased with what I have accomplished in my life? Would you be proud to call me one of your descendants, realizing that I have made the most of what I have been blessed with, trying to leave the world a better place for having been here? If we could look into each other's eyes, would we see each other, or would we see our own reflection?

People in my world often say that life back in your day was so much simpler. But was it really? Did the lack of all of today's modern conveniences make life more simple for you, or did it make it more difficult? Would you be able to find adequate words of gratitude for the advances in medicine that have erased many of the diseases that took so many of your lives?

And what about your family life? Did your teen-agers get into trouble like they do today, only in different ways? Or were they too busy tending to chores to have much time to get into trouble?

Thanks for letting me share some thoughts with you. Maybe we will meet some day after this life is over.

Your 21st-century descendant,

Carol Heizer

Perhaps you would like to write a letter to your ancestors and ask them the questions you would like to have answered.

My Great-Grandfather, Jacob Frederick Deshler

Jacob was born on January 23, 1831, in Wurttemberg, Germany, and died September 2, 1912, in Newport, Washington County, Ohio. He was the third son named after his father, the other two brothers dying in infancy. Jacob learned a trade as a tanner in Monroe County, Perry Township, Ohio, while living in the home of Israel Lentz (according to the 1850 census). On August 16, 1852, Jacob married Catharina Semon who was born in 1833 and died May 12, 1872. She is buried in New Matamoris, Ohio, and her tombstone is chiseled in German. Catharina bore Jacob seven children – 6 boys and 1 girl.

After Catharina's death, Jacob married my Great-Grandmother, Leah Anna McCardell who then bore him eleven more children, born approximately two years apart. My grandfather, Carroll Donald Deshler (after whom I am named), was third from the last of her children, so he does not have a lot of memories of his older siblings.

One thing that I thought strange about my grandfather was that he ALWAYS had to sit on the end of a pew or bench near an exit, and I never understood until one day I asked my grandmother about it. She told me, that as a boy, Grandpap had stood outside the family home hearing his mother screaming as she burned to death inside the structure. What a terrible memory for anyone to deal with, especially a child. He carried a lifelong fear of entrapment indoors. Out of consideration and love for Grandpap, I never mentioned to him what I knew.

Family records indicate that Jacob was nearly seven feet tall and that he served in the Special Guard of the German King. Family tradition says that he was born on the grounds of the palace. He came to America on the ship *Fulton* through the port of New York.

The Fulton continued in Trans-Atlantic service until 1861 when she was chartered by the U.S. Government and used as a transport ship during the Civil War. She was sold for scrap in 1870. The ship was built by the New York and

Havre (France) Shipping Line and Steam Navigation Company in 1855. Her sister ship was the *Arago*.

A few weeks ago I was in one of my favorite "jewels to junk" shops when the owner and I began to have a casual conversation. At about the same moment, I looked across the aisle and spotted what I knew was a German beer stein. I made a comment to the owner about it, saying it was different from many others I had seen. His next comment stopped me cold in my tracks. "Yeah, a guy brought in several family pieces the other day and said they were from Wurttemberg, Germany." I had to ask him to repeat it, which he did.

Imagine! The great-granddaughter of a man who died 100 years ago walks into a Louisville, Kentucky, flea market shop and finds a German beer stein made in the same area from which her great-grandparents hailed! How many times would something like that happen? Not many, I imagine!

Needless to say, the stein sits on the glass book shelves in my family room! Oh, how I wish that stein could talk! And then again … maybe I am glad it can't!

Do you have a grandparent that may have an unusual way
about them or something they do that raises a question
in your mind as to why they do that? Have you ever wondered why?
Why not ask them? Perhaps their answer will shed a lot of light on
who they are or why they do what they do. Take a trip into your family's
yesterdays and learn about your ancestors. You may find some very interesting information—
things that may pleasantly surprise you OR things that may shock you. Either way, they are
part of your family's past.
Wouldn't you like to know?

Ma and Pa Kesselring ... and a Trip Down Memory Lane

My family was small in numbers on my mother's side, but what I lacked in *quantity*, I made up for in *quality*. I was blessed with two wonderful grandparents into my adulthood and two **great-grandparents** until I was seven years old. And great they were – loving, caring, hard-working folks from German stock, better known as the Kesselring clan. (The picture at right was taken in 1946 when Elijah Lincoln Kesselring and Anna Eliza Bowersock Kesselring were in their 80's.)

I had only one cousin from my mother's family, and we had a true love-hate relationship. Dick was five years older than I was, and he delighted in teasing me. I loved being with him, but I hated it when he made me the object of his "big cousin – little cousin" games. But one thing Dick and I had completely in common was our love of spending time at our great-grandparents' home in Marietta, Ohio. Dick always referred to them as Grandma and Grandpa Kesselring, but I had somehow began calling them Ma and Pa. That always bothered my mother because she felt those names sounded terribly disrespectful. I could not imagine what she meant, for I felt such love for them.

Many years passed, and my parents and I traveled through Marietta. They asked me if I thought I could point out Ma and Pa's house, although they were convinced I would not remember. We drove up an down many streets in the neighborhood, but nothing looked familiar ... until we turned onto a particular street. Things looked very different, and I was beginning to wonder if I could join the past and the present together.

Suddenly one house seemed to leap from its property and shout, "Hey! Stop! Remember me?" I knew. I knew it was Ma and Pa's house. A lot of structural changes had been made, but I knew. I knew! Beyond the shadow of a doubt! I knew! There seemed to be an invisible bond between that house and me!

The open farm land across the street now housed a subdivision, and I wondered if the people living there had any idea that two kids sitting on their great-grandparents' front porch had watched the sun set over that field many years ago.

The little country store down the street was also gone, and in its place stood a new home. Somehow that home didn't seem to belong there ... I wanted the store to be there – that little country business where folks gathered to chat and pass the time of day.

Dick and I were city kids, and we knew nothing about *country* living. I guess Ma forgot that the day she invited us to come along to the chicken house when she collected what would become the evening meal. When she placed that chicken on the tree stump and lopped off its head with her hatchet, I was not prepared to see the body go running around the yard. In fact, I was not prepared to see a chicken die in any form or fashion! To this day, I can still remember screaming, "Ma! Ma! You didn't kill it! It's still alive!"

Poor Ma. She instantly realized her error in allowing me to watch. She snatched me up in her arms, hustled me into the house, and lovingly attempted to explain the physical reality of what I had just witnessed. But I think Ma regretted that incident until the day she died. I loved that dear old lady more than I can put into words, but I **never** went near that chicken coop again. Come to think of it, she never *asked* me to go again.

Ma and Pa loved mashed potatoes, and the family could count on having them at nearly every evening meal. When Ma would begin peeling the potatoes, Dick and I would suddenly appear out of nowhere. We knew we were not to ask for the raw potatoes, so we merely stood by Ma, knowing she would offer us the first two peeled potatoes.

Sometimes we would have one or more strangers in our midst, as the town vagrants knew that Ma had a tender spot in her heart for the less fortunate. She would never give them money, for she would not contribute to any unsavory habits in which they might indulge, but she would always feed them. And she always made them feel part of the family.

Pa passed away first on January 12, 1951, having spent his life as a farmer and carpenter. He and Ma were married on January 27, 1886, when she was 18 and he was 22. He made a kitchen table and chairs as his wedding gift to her, and I am privileged to have the only remaining chair in existence. Ma never worked outside the home, instead holding down the fort and raising her five children who filled her life and her days.

Ma was never the same after Pa's death, and she died on April 18, 1952. The lady who had meant so much to me and with whom I had shared so many good memories, was buried on April 22 of that year, my seventh birthday!

If I had the power to turn back the clocks of time, I would rewind them to the time when Dick and I sat on our great-grandparents' front porch, listening to the crickets across the road and watching the sun tuck itself into bed for another night's rest.

Think about to your earlier days and recall a special time you spent with a member of your family. What were the circumstances surrounding the memory? What made it special in your memory? Close your eyes and try to re-live it in your imagination—complete with the sights and sounds or smells that made it special.

Cousin George Armstrong Custer

Dear Cousin George,

Although we've never met, I know a great deal about you from my research, and the more I learn about you, the more intrigued I become!

Your ancestors Paulus and Gertrude followed some of the first families from Germany to America where they wanted a better life for their families and descendants.

Five generations later, you arrived as an early Christmas gift to your parents, Emanuel (a farmer and blacksmith) and Marie, in December of 1839. But sadly, both of them outlived you – a tragic experience for any parent. Your father named you after a local minister, for he hoped you would eventually become part of the clergy.

While in college, you and a classmate carried coal to pay for your room and board. After graduation, you taught school in Ohio. You were admitted to West Point Academy in 1858 where you graduated last in your class, regularly accumulating many demerits for misconduct in each of your four years there. You came very close to expulsion every year! Were you merely testing the system, or were you slow at maturing? In spite of your less-than-positive history at the Academy, you were given an officer's rank when the Civil War broke out, due to the need for all potential officers. In spite of your marred Academy past, you achieved military success both as a Union Officer and a highly effective Cavalry Commander.

At age 25, you married Libby – whose father disapproved of you because you were the son of a blacksmith. Two years after your marriage, you traveled to New York City where you explored options in the railroad and mining industries. I cannot decide if you were a man of many talents or a lost soul searching for some illusive dream!

While you seemed to be the epitome of the military "man's man," I simply cannot understand why you liberally sprinkled your hair with cinnamon-scented hair oil! That seems to be the ultimate contradiction! As I said previously, the more I learn about you, the more I become intrigued by your character.

You died as the result of two bullet wounds – one in your left temple and one above your heart. I have often wondered if you died instantly, or if you had time to realize that your life was slipping away. If you had a few precious moments of life left in you, were your thoughts of your wife and parents, or was your mind focused on how the history books would treat you? Some historians have referred to you as "brilliant," while others offered their evaluation of you as a "fool."

You were initially buried on the battlefield where you died, but your remains were later moved to the nationally-known West Point Academy cemetery. You might be interested to know that six different states have counties named in your honor, while several towns throughout the country bear your name. You would also be proud of your monuments that stand in your birthplace of Brumley, Ohio, and in your childhood hometown of Monroe, Michigan.

Yes, Cousin George, I am your second cousin 5x removed. But the world knows you as General George Armstrong Custer!

Your descendant,

Carol Heizer

Is there a famous person in your background? Although you may not think so, you may be in for a surprise if you begin investigating. Perhaps you may find similarities between that person and yourself. Perhaps not. But wouldn't it be fun searching your family tree?

LAQUITA Enters Through an "Open Door"

She came to my life in a usual way,
Sitting at the table next to me.
I'd never seen her before that night,
Yet I sensed something, then unknown.

The writers were asked to group into pairs –
Partnering with someone they didn't know.
Laquita and I, we became a team
In what we feel was "divine appointment."

The conversations began, the info exchanged –
Little did we know what was about to take place.
Her verse of scripture and my dream collide,
Meshing us together in a special way.

As a special surprise, she is Pickles' wife,
A friend of mine from my clowning days.
He's as nice as ever with his sense of humor,
And they make such a lovely couple.

But back to Laquita's and my time together,
We laughed and laughed at the things we shared –
Our silly thoughts and crazy ideas
That are typical of writers we then decided.

Do you have a special friend that came into your life unexpectedly? Why are they special to you? What makes them different from your other friends? And have you ever told them how special they are to you? Even if you think they already know, they might truly enjoy hearing you say it.

NATURE

The Rainbow's Charm

I stand and gaze at the prism-like nature of the rainbow and wonder at its charm. It seems to cast a wonderfully magic spell over the area as I take in the beauty of its iridescence and quietness. Though as silent as an unspoken word, that glorious burst of color shouts its beauty with an unseen intensity

My rainbow – yes, MY rainbow. Is that such audacious pride? I do not believe so, for it was sent for me to enjoy – both for its creation and for its Creator! Such a thing of beauty! Its quietness, its iridescence, and its beauty seem more than my finite mind can comprehend. Oh, but my spirit and my heart understand it clearly.

And then I realize the greater significance of the rainbow. It must have both sunshine and rain to exist. I knew that information before, a bit of knowledge tucked away in my thinking from long-ago studies of atmospheric elements in science class. But now – this very moment – it surfaces with a new realization.

At this moment in time when millions of people across the globe are going about their daily chores and world-wide events are taking place simultaneously, I feel completely alone in the universe as my entire being absorbs this new fact takes root within me.

My life can be as light and cheerful as a summer day, or my life can be as dark and dreary as a thunderstorm. But until my life has experienced both the sunshine and the rain, it may not be of true value to either myself or others. I must have experienced the "rain" to understand the depth of pain or suffering that mankind often experiences. And I must have experienced the sunshine to understand that affliction often does not last a lifetime – that we can rejoice in the pleasant memories of days gone by, and that we can take comfort in the fact that the suffering will usually pass – both in endurance and intensity.

And so as I stand and gaze at the prism-like nature of the rainbow and wonder at its charm, I see the multi-faceted aspects of my own life and begin to appreciate the beauty that God is creating within me to be used for His Kingdom – both here on Earth and in the Heavenly Kingdom to come.

The Mountains Rise

Those rugged mountains are tall and strong
As they reach toward the sky and Heaven above,
And they ask nothing of man so weak and frail.
They speak of the Creator's love.

How we love their beauty and rugged trails
Where we often find a lonely flower,
And wonder how it survived its struggling life.
Fragile life grows in granite by God's mighty power.

The animals, too, they have found their home
Upon the peaks and in the crannies below,
And we wonder how they ever survive.
It seems both man and nature is their foe.

And so there they are, those mountains rise
Up from the earth and waters deep,
While the earth is quiet and stands so still.
The waterfall music puts them all to sleep.

Listen to the Rocks

The afternoon was spent sitting atop a boulder jetting out from the mighty rushing water of a mountain stream. The water was as frozen liquid, and its coldness bit into my feet like a bear's teeth. The water's thundering roar seemed to drown out all other sounds as it stampeded its way down the rocky trail. Nothing seemed to exist except the brilliant blue sky, the fluffy white clouds, the blowing trees, the foaming water, the rocks, and me. And I began listening to the rocks.

I listened as they told their tales of old – how they were part of the life-giving source of drinking water for both man and beast; how some of them had been dislodged from their original homes by the rushing water and trembling earth; how their features had changed over the years by the force of the water constantly flowing over and around them.

Some of the rocks spoke of the comfort and warmth that were provided by the thick blanket of lush moss covering them. Some of the rocks shared their sense of pride at possessing such smooth, symmetrical beauty, while others boasted of their sharp ruggedness. Some of them remembered their pleasure at seeing the beautiful trout passing through their area, while other spoke of their sense of satisfaction at providing protection for the little stones lying at their base. One rock in particular shared its sense of enjoyment for providing a safe resting place for the tangled piece of driftwood that had somehow safely lodged against it. This rock felt a particular sense of responsibility for keeping its visitor secure, providing a wonderful contrast to the surrounding rocks and waters. One family of rocks explained their hospitality in providing a welcome retreat for the entwining mass of tree roots in their midst.

Finally the rock upon which I sat spoke. It expressed its delight that one would venture so far out into the rushing water and soak in the wonders of nature. Most folks, it said, stayed closer to the shore and the safety of soil. As I continued to sit and permitted my mind to drift into freedom, it was as though all the rocks began giving up their stories. They had finally found one who could, and *would*, take the time to allow a relationship to develop. As the thunderous water continued pouring around on all sides, I could sense the thoughts and dreams the rocks had absorbed over the centuries.

From the rocks, I heard the fears and uncertainties of the pioneers as they hacked and chopped their way through the mountain's dense growth – and the

fatigue those men and women must have felt as they saw yet another rocky, rushing stream, they must cross. I heard the delight of the children as they had joyfully jumped from one rock to another, apparently defying the laws of gravity and slippery surfaces.

I heard the dreams of newlyweds as they had romantically slipped away from the crowds to find their own temporary paradise – ready to embark on life together, feeling so prepared to face the world as a team, yet so completely oblivious to the trials that lie ahead. I heard the relaxation of parents as they briefly paused on the rocks and escaped the cares of everyday life and the anxieties of raising a family.

I heard the questions of middle-aged folks as they found rocks closer to the shore and snatched a few moments from the hectic world in which they functioned. These folks recalled the time in their younger years when they, too, would have ventured further into the rapids. Now they were aware of their declining agility when rock-hopping. I heard the sudden quietness within their homes since the children had left the nest – the quietness that once was so desired, and now seemed so overwhelming. I heard the uncertainty these folks were feeling as they neared retirement and suddenly had questions as to the adequacy of their financial preparations for that inevitable event.

But perhaps the saddest of all, I heard the concerns of older ladies and gentlemen who had already experienced the onset of medical problems. I heard the concern of how they would cope with those problems, both physically and mentally. Even greater than the concern, I heard the anticipated loneliness that the remaining spouse would endure after the loss of their beloved partner. But above their concern and anticipated loneliness, I heard the gratitude and appreciation for a love shared over the years – a love that had endured the daydreams and nightmares, the pleasures and the pains, the ideal and real of daily life.

As I quietly, almost reverently, left the place that had become so very special and personal to me during the afternoon, I continued to listen to the rocks. As I walked further away from my unique and distinctive place among the rocks and drew closer to the hustle and bustle of routine daily life, the rock's voices became fainter and fainter. Yet as I turned for a final farewell, I faintly heard one of them say, "Please come back again." I assured them that this day had been so rich in learning and compassion that I would be back often.

Another spoke and said, "Perhaps if we are patient, others will come along and listen to us."

Have you ever taken time from your busy schedule to walk out into the world around you and listen to nature and absorb its beauty? Listen. Really listen. And come back refreshed.

The Quiet Creek

The little creek I often visit
Rarely makes a sound
As it makes its way
Through the land and around.

I watch the leaves as they blow in the wind
And hear the birds as they sing their song.
As I visit this creek when my soul is troubled
Suddenly there seems to be nothing wrong.

I sit by myself enjoying the peace
As I shut out the world and its heavy weight
To watch the rocks that mark the path
As the water flows down both crooked and straight.

It's my quiet creek
Where I often go
In summer - the rain
In winter - the snow.

*Is there a special place in your world
where you can go and find the time,
space, and peace to be quiet within
your spirit to find the refreshment
that you need?*

The Lonely Tree

The boat sped by that lonely tree
By the deep blue water's edge.
I asked him to stop; I wanted to look.
"It's just an old dead tree," he said.

But I saw more – the beauty there
Somehow calling me to stop and listen.
"I've a story to tell," it whispered to me –
A story you'll like – perhaps learn from.

"Can we finish the ride?" he asked me then.
"Not quite yet," I answered back.
"But what do you see in that old dead tree?"
"I'm not sure, but there's beauty there."

And then I saw it, all at once I knew
It wasn't just that lonely tree.
The landscape theme all rolled into one –
Each component added its worth.

The crystal blue water flowing quietly by;
The sturdy bark on the leafless tree.
The surrounding greenery growing strong;
The ice blue sky giving its glorious light.

Life of the Rainforest Rainbow Lorikeet

He was nearing his beloved rainforest home in Australia, and his heart filled with warmth as he neared his tree. He had been away only a few days, but it had been far too long. He cherished the lush green growth of his rainforest, and he treasured the quietness that allowed him thinking time. Sometimes he entertained many thoughts—sometimes only a few. But these times were very special as he relived his life through his memories.

He felt so blessed to have been born into the aviary species, for he had two means of natural transportation—his wings and his feet. If one temporarily failed, he could rely on the other. And he had been doing this for—how many years now? Oh, well, no matter. His date of birth didn't matter. He was part of the rainforest, and time was a continuum. He felt so sorry for those poor humans—they were so bound by their watches, clocks, and timepieces. He had such freedom that humans never experienced. They seemed to live by their calendars. But not him—he relied on Mother Nature to tell him what he needed to know.

He experienced the adventures that each day brought him. He enjoyed the positive incidents and stored them in his book of pleasantries for future delight. He remembered the sweet pollen and nectar from flowers and his brush-tipped tongue that gave easy access to such goodies. He remembered the occasional fruit in which he indulged. He remembered the many occasions in which he rested his feet on the logs covered with the ever-so-soft mosses. He remembered the marvelous baths in the cup-shaped fronds of the stag horn fern—and how delightful the freshly fallen rainwater felt. He remembered the various sizes and shapes of twigs he occasionally needed for remodeling or enlarging his home. There seemed to be no end to his pleasant memories.

He also valued the more painful experiences, for it was through these periods that he learned life's greatest lessons. He stored this learning in his mind, focusing on the lesson rather than the pain, for he was far too busy living today to dwell too much on yesterday.

Only he knew his heart and mind, and he kept these ponderings to himself. They were too personal to share with others.

But what he COULD and DID share with others was his beautiful plumage—those bright rainbow-colored feathers that all the birds envied so. To him, each color represented an aspect of his life. The red represented his passion for life, and the blue represented his frequent sense of relaxation in the rainforest atmosphere. The green represented his personal growth as he grew older and wiser. The yellow represented the caution he occasionally exercised in his quest for survival, and the purple represented his sense of royalty at being such a special bird. The orange represented his wealth of gold at living in such a wonderful climate, and the white represented his sense of purity at never having been affected by the human lifestyle.

Such pity he felt for the poor humans he heard off in the distance as they trekked down the beaten paths into his world. They saw only the peripheral of his world, but he was glad for that because he knew their nature. If they knew what lie beyond their path, they would tramp their way into his paradise and attempt to "civilize" his wonderful native world.

Yes, he had been away only a few days, but it had been too long. He was home now in his beloved rainforest home, his heart warm and full for all he was—and all he had—and all he experienced. How blessed he was to be a Rainbow Lorikeet living in the rainforest.

INSPIRATION

The Innocence of Childhood

They know not hate
Nor rage nor crime.
They look at love,
At smiles—not time.

They take at face
Your love so fair.
They feel your love,
They know you're there.

They trust you now,
They'll trust you then.
Wherever you are,
Wherever you've been.

Children have an innocence –
It can't be betrayed.
You supplied them with trust,
A trust that stayed.

Is there a child in your life whose innocence you can help protect?

A Touch from the Lord

Lord, I am weary tonight and full of sadness –
        My husband is gone and so is my son,
Along with my babe from years ago.
        Sometimes I feel my life's nearly done.

What do I have to show for my work –
        The years I've spent in heartache and toil.
My body is tired, my spirit weak,
        I need anointing with Your precious oil.

Please speak to me now and heal my spirit –
        I know I will have the strength to go on.
Strengthen me now with Your precious oil,
        As you strengthened then your Apostle John.

I know where to turn and go for my help –
        It's always there when I feel so weak.
I must go there and seek the treasure,
        Yes, I know through Your Word you always speak.

Problems or Power

When problems come and trials burst in,
I think of my weakness and carnal sin.
I focus on pity and bodily aches
Until my heart often nearly breaks.

    The fatigue sets in and headache starts,
    The joy is gone and pleasure departs.
    I feel overwhelmed and ready to run,
    I feel my life is over and done.

        Then the light of Scripture invades my soul,
        And I see the truth that's therein told.
        I've been seeing God in the darkened shadow,
        Instead of basking in His provided meadow.

            I continue to read and study the Word ,
            His voice I'm sure I already heard.
            My spirit grows by minute and hour,
            I look at my problems in light of God's power.

When difficult times come your way, do you look at the situation and see nothing but the problem? Or do you remember the power that is available to you through Him?

Before, Behind, and Within

"For the Lord will go before you, and the God of Israel will be your rear guard."
Isaiah 52:12

He walks before me to guide my steps
    Toward the lowest valley, the steepest hill –
        Toward the deepest water, the hottest fire.
            He walks before me to guide my steps.

    He walks behind me, a Presence near
        To protect me from my enemies' darts,
            From words of foes, and Satan's arrows.
                He walks behind me, a Presence near.

        He walks within me to help me grow,
            To steady my soul, impart His Word,
                To make known His will and teach me trust.
                He walks within me to help me grow.

Limitless Protection

The Lord is my rock –
Strong and solid through all life's strife,
Never shaking and never faltering.
He's my stead in all of life.

The Lord is my fortress –
To Him I can forever and always run,
Keeping me often from Satan's attacks
Guiding me always 'til my race is done.

The Lord is my shield –
Holding me hourly with His outstretched arm,
Going before me as a mighty protector.
Keeping me daily from needless harm.

The Lord is my horn –
Always having his might and power,
Yet also having his love and grace.
He's my safety through every hour.

The Lord is my stronghold –
Seeing on high my hurting woes,
Yet having me to struggle as need demands.
He's the victory over all my foes.

*Do you see Him as the Rock
within your life upon which
you can stand when the sands
around you seem to be shifting?*

Sin to Salvation

Her life was a shambles and full of sin,
And she was disturbed without and within.
She knew He offered a better way,
Yet she always wanted to have her say.

    She dabbled in things she knew were wrong,
    And she used foul language even in song.
    She cheated people of their rightful money,
    Yet joked about it and thought it funny.

    When telling a story she always lied,
    But she wanted to stop and always tried.
    Her thoughts would race and her mouth would run,
    Yet every time another lie done.

    She even stole from her very best friend,
    And while she did it, kind words she'd send.
    She knew her friend had more than needed.
    Yet the inner warnings she never heeded.

But then one day she met the Savior,
And she knew His love would never waver.
She accepted His gift – the Gift of Salvation,
And she knew in her heart she was a new creation!

Why, Lord?

In dealing with others, I ask You, Lord,
Why does the way of the wicked prosper?
Why do the faithless live at ease?
Why do you not punish them, Lord,
Knowing You are a God of law?

Why do they live and have wealth untold—
Wealth they've taken from many oppressed?
I don't understand why You're waiting, Lord.

In dealing with me, I ask You, Lord,
Why I suffer and live in pain?
Why do I lack the things I desire?
Why do You not reward me, Lord,
Knowing You are a God of love?

Why have I suffered my personal loss—
The loss of my husband, precious children?
I don't understand what You're teaching, Lord.

I understand now; I see the truth.
I want justice for others, but mercy for me.
Thank You, Lord, for showing me YOU!

In the Still of the Night

In the still of the night
Is the ticking clock,
My jumbling thoughts,
Another day over –
Another day done

I'm one day closer
To greeting the Lord,
To touching His hand,
To seeing His feet –
Another day done.

He sends me to battle
To engage in the struggle,
He wins the war,
But I must fight –
Another day done.

I look back o'er the day
And wonder how,
He loves me still,
Another day over –
Another day done.

*Do you take the time each day
to thank Him for the continued
guidance and protection He provides
each day, even when things do not
go the way you had planned or hoped?*

II Chronicles 7:14

"If my people who are called by my name, will humble themselves and pray and seek my face and turn from their wicked ways, then I will hear from heaven and will forgive their sin and will heal their land."

I am called by Your name and saved by His blood –
I am Your child, and You are Abba.
Thus, I make my petition before Your throne
On this sunny day in the early Fall.

I humble myself , though it's very hard,
For I tend to be pleased with my earthly works.
Yet I know that all my talent is a gift from You –
So take the pride and give me You.

I pray to You, Most Heavenly Lord,
Knowing You hear and always answer –
Sometimes "yes" and sometimes "no,"
At other times, it's "Not just yet."

Lord, I seek Your face I have not seen.
And the face of Jesus with those tender eyes,
Battered and bruised upon the cross
On that lonely hill we call Golgotha.

Father, give me the strength and strong desire
To turn from my worldly, wicked ways –
To rather immerse myself in Your ways
And know Your will is wrought in my life.

> Lord, You have promised in Your ancient covenant
> To hear and forgive and heal our land.
> So I come to You this important day,
> Pledging my part and promising my best.
>
> Oh, dear Lord, begin a revival in our hearts today
> And let that revival spread over our land.
> Heal our land as no man can
> And bring us to You in these latter days.

Help for Today, Hope for Tomorrow

Today is the day I am living now,
With every hour passing quickly by.
I see my need in most situations,
For it has now quietly come to pass.

I do not want to waste my time
Concerned over things I cannot control.
I have not the wisdom to solve the riddles,
Nor the patience to think them through.

Then I remember the age-old truth
That He is my help for every today.
He knew this day before it began
And has my life in the palm of His hand.

Tomorrow is the day I will be living then,
With every hour passing quickly by.
I shall not worry about it now,
For it has not yet come to pass.

Needless worries I've spent in the past
Over things that never occurred.
Then I knew my worthless mistake —
Wasting time over "never" things.

I had forgotten the age-old truth
That He is my hope for every tomorrow.
He sees that day before it begins
And has my life in the palm of His hand.

Do you ever find yourself spending your energy regretting the past and worrying over the future? Take time to realize that, you cannot change the past or control the future. Instead — give yourself to focusing on today!

That Old Rugged Cross

The rough and timbered hand-hewn tree,
Made into a cross for crucifixion –
A symbol of death, of suffering, and shame
Standing upon a nearby hill.

T'was carried through Jerusalem,
The narrow streets of the city.
Some citizens looked toward the cross,
While others looked away.

"Another on their way to death," they'd say
And then return to their various tasks.
Too often this scene they'd seen,
So nothing seemed so strange.

Known by townsfolk as Via Dolorosa
From Latin, "The way of Grief, the way of Suffering."
The way of death, two thousand feet-
The torturous turns, one after another.

The scene was repeated many times
Until one day that narrow street
Became the path of God's own Son
As He carried the cross to old Golgotha.

They nailed His hands, they nailed His feet,
They gave Him gall, they speared His side.
They mocked His name and took His clothes.
They thought they'd won when He breathed His last.

But the world would soon know His death was divine!

The veil was torn from top to bottom,
The sky went dark as midnight black.
The people started and shook with fear
As they soon realized that Man was God.

The blood that ran was like no other.
It was His sacrifice for man
To live eternally with Him –
That blood upon that hand-hewn tree.

The Love of God

THE LOVE OF GOD – such a short little phrase –
Only four little words from beginning to end.
Yet when you consider the heartaches around,
Oh, the deep wounds that those words can mend.

    Those words can reach the highest star
    And span into the deepest sea.
    That love can reach to the far-off lands
    Or touch the very heart of me.

    THE LOVE OF GOD – so rich and pure –
    That perfect love that man can know.
    Far greater than any earthly wealth
    One can have in this earth below.

That love can reach to the blackest heart
And cleanse the dirtiest sinful mind.
NO greater compassion is there anywhere
Than THE LOVE OF GOD He allows us to find.

Knowledge and Wisdom

The facts of science,
    The numbers of math,
        The symbols of elements,
            The words of language –

Oh, the knowledge man has gained.
It is everywhere in the land of the living!

The images of literature,
    The mores of society,
        The principles of religions,
           The facets of law –

Oh, the knowledge man has gained.
It is everywhere in the land of the living!

The medicines of doctors,
    The procedures of surgeons,
        The strategies of lawyers,
           The directions of teachers –

Oh, the knowledge man has gained.
It is everywhere in the land of the living!

    Knowledge comes from often reading
    Books and magazines and papers of old
    Found in libraries and used book stores.

The love of the Father,
    The words of the Son,
        The acts of the Spirit –
           That is the beginning of wisdom.

Oh, the wisdom man can have.
It cannot be found in man alone.

Wisdom comes from Heaven above
As God speaks His Word
And man obeys.
The fear of the Lord is the beginning of wisdom!

I Hadn't Counted the Cost

I wanted the beauty –
But not the pain;
The glory –
But not the trial.
I wanted the rose –
But I hated the thorns.

I hadn't counted the cost.

I didn't know
The source of strength;
I hadn't thought –
The fount of power.
I wanted the rose –
But I hated the thorns.

I hadn't counted the cost.

But then I knew
The spring of stamina;
The thorns gave force –
They provided might.
I wanted the rose –
And I loved the thorns.

I had counted the cost.

The Grave

The grave is such a solemn place
Where no one laughs and no one smiles.
Sadness seems on every side
As families trace the love ones' miles.

    The grave is such a desolate place
    Where nothing grows 'cept little grass.
    Sometimes the little flowers fade
    As children try to quickly pass.

The grave is such a tragic place
Where regrets are voiced and 'pologies' made.
Heartbreak seems on every side
As loved ones through their sorrow wade.

    The grave is such a deathly place
    Where only flesh and bones lie still.
    Deafening silence all around
    As others attempt their heart to fill.

The grave is such a quiet place
Where tears and dreams flow forth as one.
Agony surrounds this piece of earth
As each one knows what's done is done.

    The grave is such a final place
    As seen from an earthly view.
    Our Father in Heaven sees only a door
    Which we will be passing through.

The grave is such a GLORIOUS place
Where earthly life 'tis finally o'er.
Rejoicing's heard from all around
As Heaven opens and blessings outpour!

OUR WORLD

An Emotional World We Live In

The world is moving at a hectic pace,
    People scurrying at frightening speeds –
        Rarely taking time to think
            Or ponder their current affairs.

These beings – we call them humans,
    Yet inhumane in this crazy world –
        In what they expect their bodies to give
            On a daily basis not regarding health.

They struggle with uncertainty,
    Never knowing what
        Those around them demand
            Or expect without even telling them.

They struggle with fear,
    Alarmed at the fast-changing world –
        Wondering if they can compete
            Or win in this maddening contest.

They struggle with dismay,
    At reading of hate and sorrow
        In the daily newspaper
            They sometimes try to avoid.

But a select few –
    They survive and function quite well
        Through knowing their true source
            Of daily renewal and strength.

On the Deck of the Ship

Let me stand here and pretend I need not leave.
Let me go deeper into the depth of the sea.
I have seen another world of quiet and serenity
That escapes those on the noisy land.

Let me remember the smell of fresh sea air,
The sound of tossing, turbulent waves,
Seeing the hues of the sky's bright rays,
The rolling of the ship as it lulls me to sleep.

Let me remember the brilliance of the stars,
The face of the moon in the darkest night,
The whitecaps of water as they wave goodbye.
Let me remember the last moments

of MEMORIES!

Do you take time from your busy life to create those special memories? It does not have to be aboard a cruise ship, or on a sandy beach. It can be anytime—anywhere—with a loved one or a pet—or even my yourself. Being alone does not equal loneliness. Would you like to know yourself better.

A Quiet Sunday Afternoon

Sarah's asleep, and so is Jake;
The clock ticks loudly, the rain falls softly.
The TV is off, and so is the music;
I sit alone with my many thoughts.

Lunch is over, the dishes done;
All is quiet, except in my mind.
No chores to be done, all is ready;
I find myself beginning to drift.

I travel to the past of days gone by;
I wonder what the future holds.
I cannot know what lies in store;
I only have today to count.

Some loved ones are gone, they're in my heart;
As long as remembered, they're never gone.
So I'll take my thoughts and move on forward;
Yesterday is past, tomorrow's not here.

I'll take what I'm given – and make it the best!

Are you willing to make the best of bad situations that come into your life? To take difficulty or hurt and learn to make yourself a better person?

The Unexpected Visitors

My day had been especially busy, and it was not a convenient time for visitors. But she arrived, nonetheless, with her two children. Young ones always seem to give us adults a new view of the world, and these two young ones were no different. They enjoyed the fresh air, the warm sun, and the softly blowing breeze. They even enjoyed the snacks that were offered. They were curious and active, but they stuck close to Mama. Somehow they knew that she was their security. We call it *natural*, but it is still interesting to observe, particularly when the young ones periodically glance in Mama's direction, just to make sure she is still there. Each of the little ones ventured into his own space for a time enjoying the surroundings, but he would then return to his sibling – just to be certain that brother hadn't found something more interesting!

They stayed longer than I expected, but it was still a nice visit – especially when I stopped to remember that sometimes the nicest things in life come in unexpected packages and at unanticipated moments.

From a distant part of the house, the dog suddenly became aware of the afternoon visitors on the premises, and he quickly voiced his dissatisfaction with their presence by wailing in that unmistakable Beagle howl.

Being started and terribly frightened, the doe and her two little fawns leaped into the surrounding woods, finding safety and security in the thickets and underbrush.

Do you see surprise visitors,
be they human or otherwise, as
an interruption in your day? Or do
you see them as unexpected blessings?

The Election

The election is drawing closer,
And Christians are concerned.
Will the right man be elected,
Or will the wrong one be confirmed?

Will God's most gracious hand
Bless our land as we have known?
Or will we reap the sorrow
Of the sinful seeds we've sewn?

We've pushed Him out of every place,
Then asked why evil thus came in.
We go to Him in times of trouble,
But forget Him in the times we win.

We use His name in profane ways,
And joke about His Son.
Yet then we panic and pray aloud
When all things seem to come undone.

And yet we know within our hearts
God's plan will surely be.
Regardless of the man who wins,
God's will we will surely and certainly see.

Sunset at Sea

I enjoy the beauty
of sunset at sea
as I near the end
of an eventful trip.
The sun has blessed us
each day of our journey.
But now it is time
for the sun to rest.

It lowers itself into bed
and quietly pulls the cover
of the horizon over its head.

The WORLD from the TOP of the ALPS

The shout of the wind,
yet the whisper of snow.

The strength of the mountain,
yet the frailty of man.

The longevity of rock,
yet the brevity of life.

The steadfastness of reality,
yet the fickleness of emotion.

The desire to stay,
yet the need to leave.

White Sands and Waving Palms
(Roatán, Honduras)

I started across the white board walk,
Headed for the water, that beautiful blue,
The hut at the end was where I could rest,
But before I arrived I soaked in the beauty.

The breeze of the palms blowing in sync
To an unheard song they were swaying to.
The songs of the birds with their tropical hues
Seemed almost too perfect to be truly real.

The white sand covered the area around,
It slipped 'tween my toes as I walked along.
I didn't mind that feel of the sand —
It felt much better than city concrete.

The wooden chairs were stained dark brown;
They looked so relaxing, I had to sit.
Nothing to do, nothing to read —
Simply to sit and soak in the rays.

But between the boards, the hut, and the sand,
My spirit took flight as I watched the clouds
And imagined myself on that royal blue water.
And sad as it was, it was time to leave.

I waved goodbye with a sigh in my heart.

A Tribute to Mount Egmont
(New Zealand)

He stands majestically against the sky,
Never speaking, yet shouting tales of
Strength and courage and steadfastness
As he stands rooted in the earth,
Reaching his peaks toward Heaven.

He has a variety of coloring —
Some are earthen tones of gray and brown rock,
Others the winter hues as he stands
Clothed in the snows of winter

Then come the wonderful colors
Of springtime attire as the
Pale lime-green daisies and wildflowers,
And green mosses clothe their host.

As do the seasons,
He is continuously transforming,
Ever-changing, yet remaining the same,
Standing majestically against the sky.

Conversing With the Tasman Sea
(New Zealand)

You permitted me to walk toward you,
    Feeling the pulsating pounding of your surf.
My toes sank into your iron ore sandy beach,
    Glistening as a black diamond field
        in the afternoon sun.

You called me to venture into your ice-cold water,
    And you rolled toward me with a frightening,
        Yet peaceful, speed.
Your liquid tongue lapped at my ankles –
    then my calves – until I could stand it no more.

You treated me to a myriad of white caps
    Atop your dark water,
Accented by your billowing gray mist
    Rising around your ruggedly beautiful boulders
        Jetting out from your thundering waters.

You invited me to linger in your surf and sand –
    To enjoy the wind in my face.
You asked me to feel your presence
    In my being as never before today –
        To merely enjoy the beauty of your bounty.

Your spirit touched my spirit
    Surpassing all words,
You asked me to feel your freedom,
    To experience your joy –
        to enjoy simply "being."

    But then, as all things must end,
        You bade me farewell,
    Reminding me of other goals to achieve,
        Other tasks to undertake –
            and to remember you always.

Landing at Ben-Gurion Airport
(Tel Aviv, Israel)

I carefully step down from the white portable ramp
    That extends from the plane that brought me here.
I set foot on Israeli soil
    Or rather Israeli LAND
The sun from Ben-Gurion Airport's concrete
    Nearly blinds me as I make my descent.

This city is of finance and business and fun –
    It doesn't compete with three thousand years
Of history and time.
    Nearly everyone here comes from somewhere else.
A walk through the city will reveal its "diverse"
    From oriental to pastel pink condominiums.

The entrance to Ben-Gurion is an impressive sight
    A row of Israeli flags flying in the breeze.
The atmosphere inside is formidable,
    Actually quite tense.
There's no joking nor humor to see
    And all the soldiers have their Uzis in tow.

As military guards in perfect posture stand in every corner,
    I see their commitment to their official job –
To defend their country
    As their ancestors have done,
Their message is clear,
    "We defend our country to our dying breath."

The Holy City
(Jerusalem, Israel)

As I enter Jerusalem, the words of Psalm 122 come to mind: "I was glad when they said until me, Let us go into the house of the Lord. Our feet shall stand within thy gates, O Jerusalem. Jerusalem is built as a city that is compact together: Whither the tribes go up, the tribes of the Lord, unto the testimony of Israel, to give thanks unto the name of the Lord. For there are set thrones in judgment, the thrones of the house of David. Pray for the peace of Jerusalem; they shall prosper that love thee. Peace be in thy walls, and prosperity within thy palaces. For my brethren and companions' sake, I will now say, Peace be within thee. Because of the house of the Lord our God I will seek thy good" (NIV).

Truly, Jerusalem is a city that could not stay destroyed. It has stood over the centuries as a site of tremendous good and treacherous evil. It was here in Jerusalem where the Gospel was first preached and the Holy Spirit came at Pentecost. Yet it is also where Stephen was stoned to death and where the disciples were persecuted. It is a city that has suffered pestilence, famines, and wars...yet was referred to as the Holy Mountain.

I walk in the shade as I climb the long stone steps that lead into the Old City. These small trees offer a welcome relief from the heat, and I suddenly am asking myself if their ancestor trees lined these steps two thousand years ago. Were these steps I am now climbing here in the days of Jesus? Could He have walked the very same path I now scale?

I view the living quarters of Ethiopian monks and see their poverty-stricken living conditions. Would I survive or function in such circumstances? I feel overwhelmingly blessed, yet so unworthy of my blessings. While trying to truly take in this area, several tourists come through and "pose" for a photo. I am shocked! They walk to the far wall, take down a large wooden cross that is leaned against it, place it over their shoulder, and wait for their keepsake picture to be taken. I cannot imagine anyone posing for such a picture! Do these tourists have any idea of the suffering and humiliation associated with such an act? Do they know that such a death was reserved for the vilest of criminals? Witnessing this scene pierces my heart to its core! But the precious gift of salvation to each of us and the great price He paid speaks to my heart even more intensely.

    I visit Caiaphas' home where Jesus was kept before His crucifixion. The beauty of the gardens the blooming fragrance of the flowers, and the cleanliness of the nearby sculptures belie the inhumane acts of cruelty that are known to have taken place—in *this* place—underground.

    As I stand and stare—almost transfixed—at these walls, I sense an overwhelming burden of suffering. Am I truly hearing the screams of those dying for their faith and being tortured for preaching The Truth, or is my mind attempting to re-create the terrible scenes? Whatever the reason, I feel I will never be the same after having been here.

    As I prepare to leave this underground prison, I see a bronze statue of Jesus kneeling—His head toward Heaven and His hands bound in chains. It reminds me again of His torment in this awful place, but I rejoice in the truth of the inscription below the statue:

The Servant of the Lord
Because He surrendered
Himself to death
And was counted
Among the wicked,
while bearing the sins of
many
and interceding
for transgressors (Isa. 53:12)

God highly exalted Him
And bestowed on Him
The name
above every other name.
(Phil.2:9)

Pray for the peace of Jerusalem!

The Garden of Gethsemane
(Outside Jerusalem, Israel)

I visit this sacred place and enjoy the beauty of the area—the blooming roses, the stone walkways, the flowering shrubs, and the old gnarled olive trees that exhibit such beauty in their ruggedness and twistedness. Some of them are so bent, they are supported by stone pillars that have been constructed for their support.

The Garden's beauty contrasts Jesus' suffering that took place there. Could one of these trees be the very one under which He prayed the night before His crucifixion?

The olive tree becomes hollow as it ages and, as it splits in the center, new shoots begin. I realize that the trees' life cycles are representative of life in many respects, especially the spiritual aspect. Only when we die out to ourselves can true life spring forth.

I wonder—what must Jesus have felt as He and the disciples neared the Garden. Why did He tell all the others except Peter, James, and John to stay at the outer edges of the Garden? Was it because only they formed the inner circle of Jesus' closest friends? Did He feel He needed their love and their support?

Did the anguish increase as He went deeper into the Garden? Did He feel more alone with each step He took? Did His steps become slower and heavier? Did His shoulders stoop lower the further He went? Did His hands and feet begin to ache in anticipation of the nails being driven into them? I shudder as I ask myself, "What does it feel like to have a nail pounded into your wrist? Into your foot?" Was He even aware of His outward surroundings as He approached the innermost part of the Garden?

When Jesus found His three closest friends—His confidantes, the men whom He thought He could depend upon the most—sleeping, the hurt He must have felt! The utter loneliness. The separation from human companionship and loyalty. Did He weep again at what He saw?

I am overcome by the history of two thousand years ago that is playing itself out in the deepest recesses of my mind and heart. I cannot seem to comprehend it all, yet I feel completely surrounded by it. I realize that my breathing is becoming more difficult, and I sit completely motionless as I feel engulfed by all I am experiencing.

Sitting in the Garden, I am overwhelmed by the life and influence of the God/Man we know as Jesus. His agony, His submission, His commitment to do the Father's will, and all the Fruits of the Spirit He displayed while on earth.

As I find a place to sit off by myself, I realize the intense quietness of the moment. I look toward Jerusalem and see the Eastern Gate—the gate through which Christ will come in His Second Coming. The gate has remained sealed since His days upon Earth, and the Arabs want it to remain so. They believe that keeping it sealed will prevent the Messiah from returning. How sad—to believe that human endeavor can prevent the will of God from taking place. Yet do we – do I – not occasionally vainly attempt to obstruct what we sometimes feel God has called us to do?

The Sea of Galilee
(Tiberias, Israel)

As I contemplate the great significance of this area, both to the world and to Christian history, I realize the word "sea" is a misnomer, for it is not truly a *sea*. Rather, it is an inland body of fresh water (even though the surface is below sea level).

Since my hotel is just across the street from the beach, I am able to rise at 4:45 am for two mornings and have the precious opportunity to watch the sun rise over the Sea of Galilee. I thought I would be alone in my experience, but I see two other people capturing the same experience for themselves. But they go further down the beach, so we can be all alone with our thoughts.

As I sit by myself in these early morning moments, I wonder—are the large rocks I see perhaps the ones Jesus sat upon? Are the tiny pebbles I pick up pieces of original rocks upon which Jesus sat? Did He ever sit here early in the morning as I am doing now and simply ponder the world around Him or the world above Him to which He was soon to return?

I think of when Jesus calmed the storm upon these very waters. I can only imagine the disciples' astonishment that His command, "Peace! Be still!" in Matthew 4:39 would calm the wind and waves. And imagine their terrified shock in Matthew 14:25-26 when they beheld someone walking on the water—thinking it was a ghost—only to realize it was Jesus Himself.

Then there's Peter—wonderful Peter—who is so much like many of us (vacillating from one extreme to the other). Peter's faith allowed him to walk on the water also at the Lord's command and, oh, what he must have been thinking as he did so. But then his human fear and lack of faith took over, and he began to sink. Only his plea to Jesus saved him from an untimely drowning.

One moment, I wonder how Peter could have doubted the Master's voice, but then I must ask myself, "If I heard Jesus' voice calling out to me to step out of the safety of a boat and plant my feet on water, would I not have fear also?"

Are you willing to trust His voice when He calls, or do you tend to rely on your own human strength and ability?

Leaving My Spiritual Homeland
(Netanya, Israel)

I stand on my balcony overlooking the Med -
    It faces the west,
        And I pray for a sunset
            To capture on film.

A military copter regularly flies overhead -
    As a routine fly-by,
        Part of the military
            Protecting her borders.

This tiny nation since the days of old -
    Has faced hatred and strife,
        Survived her wars
            And threats of extinction.

I walk along the shore at dusk -
    The sun is setting,
        And things are quiet
            As my heart is heavy.

I've been in the birthplace of my Christian faith –
    I am reluctant to leave,
        I want to re-live it
            And see it again.

The brilliant sun begins to drop –
    The water turns to shades of gold,
        And skies begin to darken
            Dark colors take over the Med.

Early in the morn the following day –
    I take one last walk along the shore,
        It is difficult walking
            In the shifting sand.

I suddenly see a cluster of flowers –
    Coming from sand and rock,
        It reminds me to always
            Bloom where you're planted.

I have no supernatural vision –
    Cannot see the future in that regard,
        But some things I certainly know
            About my faith and home in Heaven.

Fish and Chips
(London, England)

I just lost 5 hours of my life. My body says it's 2:45 am—the middle of the night. But my watch (already set for London time), says it's 7:45 am. The airport is bustling at the start of another day in jolly old England.

I cannot get used to these people driving on the "wrong" side of the road. It is confusing to my already-tired mind, especially the traffic at intersections. On the European continent, driving on the left side of the road is a result of Napoleon's influence (he was left-handed). I see these signs that say, "Flats to let." I learn that means "room for rent."

I had to have a bellboy show me how to turn on the lights. I simply had to put my room key (a plastic card) into a slot in the wall. And on came the lights! If I want the lights to STAY on, I must leave my "key" in the slot. Oh, how complicated things seem all of a sudden.

I went out for an early dinner of traditional "fish and chips" at Herford Arms Pub—a delightful little place in the true English tradition. But then, again, what other tradition would they be following? After all, this IS England.

My after-dark stroll around the area yielded some interesting experiences. The Brits drive on the "wrong" side of the road after dark just like they do during the day! That's a bit of humor, dear chap! Fresh flowers are everywhere—growing in hanging baskets, sitting in windows, people carrying them in florist paper, and vendors selling them on every corner. They add such beauty and color!

I passed a quaint little pub where the only light shining through the windows was from a single taper candle at each table. Somehow the atmosphere drifted out onto the sidewalk, almost beckoning passersby to come in and join the festivities.

I had thought I would have no difficulty understanding the English brogues, but I was definitely mistaken. I have had to ask nearly every person to repeat their comments. No longer will I consider *American* English and *English* English to be synonymous. Another lesson learned!

I wonder how the English *really* feel toward us Americans? Do they think we have no *finesse*? Do they think we slaughter the King's English? Well, I suppose I will never know.

I visited Harrod's Department Store and enjoyed a lunch of creamy pumpkin soup, bread, and water in a little café within the store. As a patron, we were given a voucher for the luxury washroom (the only one in the store). I suppose one might say it was a case of "pay to see." But if I needed to use the facility again, I needed to pay.

My day ended by enjoying a spectacular *Les Miserables* at London's famous Palace Theatre—three hours of magnificent theatrical art.

The City of Lights
(Paris, France)

After leaving Dover, England, and crossing the English Channel which is one of the busiest waterways in the world (hosting up to six hundred ships in a 24-hour period), I am finally able to rest at the Holiday Inn Pantin in the eastern part of Paris. I am able to tour the city at night and go to the second floor of the Eiffel Tower (the highest point permitted to tourists). I learn that Paris spends more on illuminating its buildings than any other city on earth and is known as *The City of Lights*.

It is raining as I stand in the Eiffel Tower trying to absorb the beauty of the city after dark. The Tower is moving in the wind, but I manage to get a few photos of "Paris at Night." I know they will not be my usual sharp focus due to the slow shutter speed, the rain, and the wind. But they will be my photos—not just a post card purchased at a nearby shop. It is totally exhilarating and breathtaking!

I learn something quite interesting about the Eiffel Tower. The city of Paris did not support Eiffel's efforts, so he built the tower with his own money. Therefore, he owned it, since the city merely gave him the land on which to build it.

The tower must be painted every seven years, and it takes four year and 50 tons of paint to complete the job. Talk about a huge undertaking!

The people here do not seem very friendly, and the cashier at the restaurant where I dine this evening tried to short-change me when he thought I do not understand French currency. I continued to hold out my hand, looking directly at him, until he realized I *did* know French currency, and I did know how to add. He then apologized for "such an honest mistake."

The following day I travel out into the country-side to enjoy the view and upon returning to Paris, it begins to *snow*—in late March, no less! Amazing! French snowflakes look just like American snowflakes! Further on in our journey, however, the snow turns to plain old rain. I suppose one might say *French* rain!

Trees line nearly every street in Paris, often accompanied by flowering bushes. The Seine River separates the city into two parts—the Left Bank (very intellectual where they ponder the mysteries of life) and the Right Bank (very commercial where money is spent and work is done).

Wealth seems to seep from every corner of the city, and I learn that France has so much gold, they cover many of their statues, outdoor ornamentation, and even parts of bridges in 14k gold leaf. Rather than being impressed by that fact, I find it sad and disheartening to realize how much food that could provide to the starving people around the world.

Homeland of My Ancestors
(Heidelberg, Germany)

I stop at a nearby department store and purchase a CD containing typical Italian, Austrian, and German music. As I play the disc and hear the songs, I want my mind to travel back to the places I have been and remember the people I have seen.

As I travel through this area, I think of my ancestors on my mother's side who came from this country—how they might have felt as they left their homeland and traveled to America so many years ago.

How would it feel—what would one think—to be preparing to leave all that was familiar and venture off into a world totally foreign to live out the rest of your life? New language new monetary system, new food, new climate, new styles of clothing, new social and religious customs—all at once? No time to adjust or gradually acclimate yourself. Jump in with both feet and hope for survival. What a courageous lot of people they were!

This Bavarian section of Germany has the greenest grass one can imagine, and the small individual communities sit nestled together in picturesque groupings, with all of the homes being similar in their cream-colored exteriors and terrra cotta colored roofs. I wonder if the tight clustering of homes somehow also represents a tightly knit relationship among the people themselves?

There are no highway billboards , so the countryside is not littered with advertising that blocks my view of the surrounding area. The heavy gray clouds make a striking contrast to the lush green fields and deep brown, newly planted soil that stretches for miles in all directions.

I toured Heidelberg Castle and, as I wandered through the halls of that ancient building, I wondered…did my ancestors ever have the opportunity to walk through these halls? Did they have the opportunity to explore these mammoth-size rooms? If they spoke as they went from room to room and, considering a sound wave never dies, could I extract their conversations from these walls if I had the right equipment? Of course, I would not be able to understand their German language. But, oh just to hear their voices!

Have you ever desired to tour the homeland of your ancestors?
Have you ever wanted to let yourself travel into their culture
and feel what they perhaps felt? To see perhaps what they saw?

The Miner
(Hartz Mountains, Germany)

Because these mountains are the highest areas in northern Germany, it attracts winter sports such as skiing that attract people from all over the world. Beautifully colored ski suits and smiling faces can be seen careening down the mountain in the almost-blinding white snow. The air is heavy with fun, excitement, and vacation days of various activities.

Another world exists in this high mountainous area of Germany, and that is the Laurenthals Gluck silver mining area. It is the oldest mining area in the world where workers also dig for copper, lead, and other minerals and ores. The main mining shaft holds an underground chapel that conducted 3:00 am services at the beginning of twelve- to fourteen-hour workdays with the closing statement of each chapel service being, "In God we go."

Early miners always carried a canary into the mines to indicate when the air quality was becoming dangerous because the bird became aware of the danger before the miners, giving the opportunity to get out before unconsciousness overtook them.

Because of how long it took to descend and ascend the mine shafts, plus the required shift time and the superstition that miners had about leaving the mine at night, many of them simply stayed in the mine during the workweek and came to the top for the weekend.

This mining area was last used in 1931 and opened to the public in 1975. Having spent only two hours in the mine, I found myself wondering how it must have been for miners to spend the majority of their time in that tunnel in the earth.

A Miner's Life

Deep in the mountain he spent his days —and sometimes his night.
The darkness, the dampness, the noise—they took their toll.
He sacrificed his eyes, his ears, his lungs, his back—
All for the good of his family.

One hour to the shaft, three hours out, and 12 hours in the mine—
But paid only for his shift.
Too much climbing—he'd spend the week in the mine—
Away from his family,
Away from his friends,
Away from sunlight,
Away from fresh air,
And life and health.

No time to be sick, he needed the money.
His family needed money,
But they needed him too.
His muscles ached, his hands were blistered.
And his back bent down.

He prayed his sons would avoid the mines—
His daughters never the wives of miners.
But in anguish he always knew they would.

Too sick he became,
Too early he died.
His children cried,
His young wife mourned.
The company profited,
So everyone accepted—
And so did we!

Life went on in the mining town—
Another day,
Another shift,
Another collapse,
Another death.
And life goes on.

The City Divided
(Berlin, Germany)

Sitting in the Hotel Agon in the former East Berlin, I wonder about the pain and suffering and separation this city once held. What was this hotel used for during those dark days? Was it empty and permitted to fall into disrepair? Or was a housing facility for East German soldiers? Did such men sit in the very room I am now enjoying?

Did perhaps a Jewish family try to find refuge here after being forced from their homes? Only the walls know for sure, and they are not talking. So I am left to my imagination to wonder about historic secrets this structure holds.

I cannot conceive of the fear and the terror of living constantly under the threat of losing home, family, freedom, and life. I wonder not only about the anxiety of the adults for themselves—but for the future of their children and grandchild, brothers and sisters, parents, older family members, and friends.

As I stood by the longest remaining section of the Berlin Wall and allowed my fingers to touch it, I thought deeply about the number of East and West Germans attempting to touch that wall, trying desperately somehow to make contact with loved ones on the other side.

How many dreams were dashed by this wall? How many prayers sent Heavenward? How many tears shed? I felt an odd sense of forlornness as I continued touching that wall, wanting to leave, yet somehow needing to stay a little longer.

What can we learn from this wall? We can give thanks that it is gone.
We can appreciate those who worked to bring freedom to this country.
We can also remember to love our families more as we feel the sadness
of separation. We can take care to keep walls of separation from dividing
us from those we love.

A City of Color
(Poznan, Poland)

The actual feel of Polish soil is no different than that of Italian soil, French soil, or English soil—but the emotional feel is quite different. It is the realization that it is the soil of a country I have never before experienced. That—and the historical significance of this country's past in relation to Hitler's quest to conquer Europe—and perhaps the world—gives me a strange, almost foreboding feeling.

The fear,
The sleepless nights,
The frightened children,
The separated families,
The uncertainty—
Who would be next?

The colorful buildings,
The hanging lowers,
The clean-swept streets,
The people meandering—
They all cover the pain of the past.

I went to see Poland today.
I greeted this lady,
I took her picture,
She gave me permission.
The smile on her face
And her easy walk—
Left me with a hope
that brightens a
dark remembrance.

The End of the Line
(Auschwitz, Poland)

"...without awareness of the past, there is no road to the future."
- Sept. 23, 1977
   Helmut Schmidt, Chancellor,
   Republic of Germany

A famous picture, seen many places—
In stores, museums, and other locales.
But I wanted my own, I took the walk—
Back down the tracks with heavy heart.

As I walked the rails could I really hear
The sobs and pleas of those dear souls?
Or was it my mind trying to listen
To the beat of my own thumping heart?

The tracks into torture:
The beginning of Hell.
Many would come.
Few would leave.
Babies torn from
The arms of their moms.
Husbands and wives
Wept goodbye.
Siblings parted,
Never to meet.
The end of life
For many here.

But some survived
And told their story.
Many couldn't believe
Humans treated humans
The way they did here.

The Woodcarving Merchant
(Wroclaw, Poland)

We met on the street but couldn't converse,
He knew no English, I knew no Polish.
My camera in hand and a few little gestures,
He got the message—I wanted his picture.

The one I called his Business Look,

The other I called "The Other Look."

Not What I Expected
(Rome. Italy)

Leaving Milan and heading toward Rome
I hear Italian music being played as I travel along.
Such a nice touch to the listening ear
As I travel through flatland and now the mountains.

It's rather like life.

> Sometimes even and uneventful
> Sometimes traumatic and troublesome.
>
> Sometimes green with growth and life,
> Sometimes brown with stagnation and death.
>
> Sometimes enjoying a downhill slide,
> Sometimes struggling a rugged climb.
>
> But ever-changing,
> Often unpredictable.

Upon arriving in Rome I am shocked,
>   For in my mind it was romantic and clean.
But it's crowded and busy and dirty,
>   Not at all like I imagined it there.

There's an auto accident every ten minutes;
>   One person killed each day in the street.
Italian drivers won't hit a mother with children,
>   So always cross the street with them.

I went to the Coliseum with lots of dread;
>   I thought I might hear the dying cries.
Or perhaps the screams of the tortured numbers
>   Who gave their lives in past centuries.

Their lives were lost 'mist horror and glee;
>   The victims' cries – the spectators' laughs
As Christians stood their ground, denied not Christ,
>   A crown of glory awaited them then.

I could not enter the Coliseum, I could not bear
>   To stand on that ancient blood-soaked ground
And look around as another curious visitor.
>   Somehow that area seemed almost sacred to me.

> *Can it be that the big, cruel*
> *city of ancient times simply*
> *lives on with a modern face?*

A City of Beauty at the Foot of the Mountains
(Innsbruck Austria)

I spend a wonderful afternoon enjoying the sights of Innsbruck, trying to absorb the beauty of the surrounding mountains. I went for a short walk after dark, crossing the bridge from our Mundshein Hotel over into the business district. I was told there is very little crime in Innsbruck, and I considered venturing further. But I decided against the idea, after all. Why ask for trouble?

Everywhere I look, I see the snow-covered mountains, and my love for them seems to grow stronger the longer I stay. Perhaps the mountains speak to me of longevity and steadfastness, of quiet and peace.

To Love the Mountain

Such an intense love within my soul for the mountains
Rising high above the ground
To a height that reaches into the clouds
And disappears into the air above.

Such a longing to go to the top
And take in the air free of humanity and care.

To walk, to look, to explore—
To see what's on the other side
And experience all its blessings.

But they are there and I am here—
And I realize perhaps we shall never meet.

Yet in my mind, the mountains and I are one,
Joined in spirit by a love I cannot explain.

The Great Wall of China

      During the building of The Great Wall, which extended over many dynasties because each emperor kept improving it, every man between the ages of 16 and 60 had to work for three months each year for the emperor to complete the wall. If a man could not work the compulsory three months yearly, he had to pay extra tax. The wall was originally started by the Zianghu (hoo) people from Mongolia in the northern part of the country. Although there is no real evidence to support this fact, tradition says that if a man died while working on the wall, he was buried within the wall.

I have read about it—I have seen pictures of it.
Now I will touch it—I will walk on it.
Forty-three hundred miles long used as a barrier
To stop invading and conquering enemies.

I can choose one of two routes—the hard or the easy.
I choose the hard to test my stamina.
I can travel to five towers or stops on the way
With fifteen hundred steps between each tower.

A handrail was there but not very useful.
Its height made for Chinese and not Americans.
The altitude was high and the steps uneven
Which made the trek all the more tiring.

The further I went, the thinner the air.
The stronger the wind, the weaker my legs.
I had to decide to go on or to stop
My body was tired, my heart said, "Go on!"

A Chinese couple and I passed several times.
They would pass me, then I would pass them.
We couldn't converse, I knew no Chinese
So we smiled and waved and gave "thumbs up."

I felt both fatigue and happy delight.
I was near the top, I had made the journey.
Just eight steps from the top
Something beautiful happened.

The Chinese couple was at the top.
She saw me coming, really tired.
She came back down and took my hand
And together we climbed the final eight steps!

No words were exchanged.
She took my hand and together we walked.
Two souls in shared kindness
Experiencing a true human bond.

The Continent—and Country of Australia
(Australia's East Coast)

The cities on the coast are beautiful and bright;
    They almost remind me of American cities.
It's hard to believe I am half a world away,
    Enjoying the sights and sounds of Aussie "land."

Busy Sydney with its stunning opera house;
    The little shops on "The Rocks" are quaint.
Manly Beach offers a dazzling view,
    While Darling Harbor welcomes the ships.

Then it's off to Melbourne and its chilly weather,
    As I visit the Shrine of Remembrance.
I am inspired at the splendor of Hotel Windsor,
    And enjoy the stores on old Bourke Street.

Soon I'll stand in the famous Alice Springs,
    Where nearby stands the astounding Ayers Rock.
It's hot and dry and far from lights,
    Yet I'll see the inky black skin of the Aborigines.

The sunsets off the well-known Gold Coast,
    Are a sight to behold in any language.
I see a few whales as they arch their backs,
    And prepare for the long journey back home.

The Outback
(Alice Springs)

This famous area of Australia's land seems so barren and void of life. I can see for miles of nothing but dirt and dried bush stick. I see no apparent source of water, no shade, and no animals scurrying around. But upon closer examination, I realize there are many forms of life here, often overlooked by my "civilized" eyes. I am astonished to see ant hills that reach four feet in height, and I watch little lizards of different types.

As I turn my thoughts from the land to the people, I see how important the ancestral beliefs are to the Aborigines. One belief they hold is the idea of "dreaming." This is a way of meditating that combines in their minds the past, present, and future. It links them spiritually to other people, nature, and their environment.

As I visit with the people who live here, I see a people who were made by the land in which they live. I come to respect their skills and knowledge when I realize that my life experiences have in no way prepared me to live with such hardship. I now truly understand that "intelligence" comes in many forms!

We can admire such groups as the Aborigines and Native Americans in their ability to live in communion with nature—not only taking from the land as needed, but also continuously giving back to the land in the way they care for their surroundings.

To look at this barren land, it is hard to imagine that these people can successfully go into the Outback and find underground water by using ancient, yet tried-and-true ancestral methods. Their coarse, hard-looking features make me initially afraid to approach them, but I find them to be rather amiable as I make myself go closer and offer them a smile. I so enjoy their Australia dialect, and part of me wishes to stay behind and learn more of their ways. Part of me thinks I might not survive the "learning curve."

WRITING and SPEAKING

The Gift Within Me

There is a muse within me that frequently makes an exit and has an audience. If I tend to ignore the request, that muse seems to set aside its polite request and makes a demand. It must come forth, it says, for it has light and insight to give. It may be about to teach a valuable life lesson that will lessen or eliminate future pain and heartache. Or it may be about to teach a priceless bit of humor to enjoy as future days bring darker clouds.

I can contact that muse at times and make my request known for a specific idea or train of thought. I may be under a deadline, or I may simply want to reduce something to paper to serve as a reminder of current thoughts. Perhaps I may want to save something special for posterity's sake. Whatever the reason, I can tap into the muse and it brings forth the desired results. Oh, how grateful I am that it is so cooperative!

Other times, that muse within me lies quietly for days or weeks or months, perhaps resting in anticipation of future work and revelation. At such times I question its reality - and whether ***if*** or ***when*** it will return. I try to go into its inner sanctum and rouse its sleep, but it often avoids my attempts. It seems to have a mind of its own, and it often likes to come and go of its own volition. That frustrates me for, after all, it lives within my soul, and that should give me power over it. But such is not the case in these particular circumstances. Oh, how frustrated I am with its stubbornness!

Then it teaches me a lesson – a lesson I shall carry with me for the remainder of my life. This muse – this wonderful muse – is a gift. It may be a gift from my genetics, or it may be a gift from my upbringing. Then again, it may be a combination of both, but regardless of its origin, it is nonetheless a gift, and I am to treasure it as I would treasure any gift. I am to thank the Giver and appreciate the gift for all its precious qualities…**this gift within me**!

Do you take time to recognize and appreciate
the gifts that the Giver has bestowed upon you?
When you do that, do you promise to use
them for Him?

ABSTRACT THOUGHTS and CONCRETE PAPER

Abstract thoughts – no form or shape –
They come from without,
Yet they come from within,
All the while beginning a life – A life of their own,
Starting to grow.

    Those abstract thoughts – they come at night,
    They come at noon.
    They even come in the early dawn
    When the mind is open to abstract thoughts.

They walk around in my busy brain
Seeking a root from which to start.
They may tip-toe quietly or stomp about,
But they always make their presence known.

    But then it begins – that arduous task
    Of putting these thoughts to concrete paper.
    How can one make the difficult change
    From unseen thoughts to readable language?

It begins with my will,
The will to achieve,
To give form and shape
To those abstract thoughts.

    So the keyboard sits quiet upon the desk,
    Waiting for action from the writer's fingers.
    Suddenly the letters start dancing on screen
    As the abstract thoughts come to concrete paper.

Writing Is Like Giving Birth

Writing begins with *wanting* to write,
    just as family begins with wanting children.
The first ideas come in scattered forms,
    just as plans for baby begin in many forms.

The ideas take shape in proper sequence,
    just as hopes and dreams for baby begin to flow.
Finally the written form begins in the brain,
    just as Mom declares, "Guess what? I'm pregnant!"

Months fly by as chosen words appear on paper,
    just as Mom grows bigger with the growing baby.
But as time goes by, the work gets harder,
    just as Mom feels greater pressure and begins to tire.

The creative writing process oftentimes will lag,
    just as Mom feels the pregnancy will never end.
There is light at the end of the writing tunnel,
    just as Mom feels the great anticipation rising.

The writing is finished and the editing complete,
    just as Mom has all in readiness and begins to wait.
The big day arrives, the work is complete,
    just as Mom cries out, "Oh, how beautiful!"

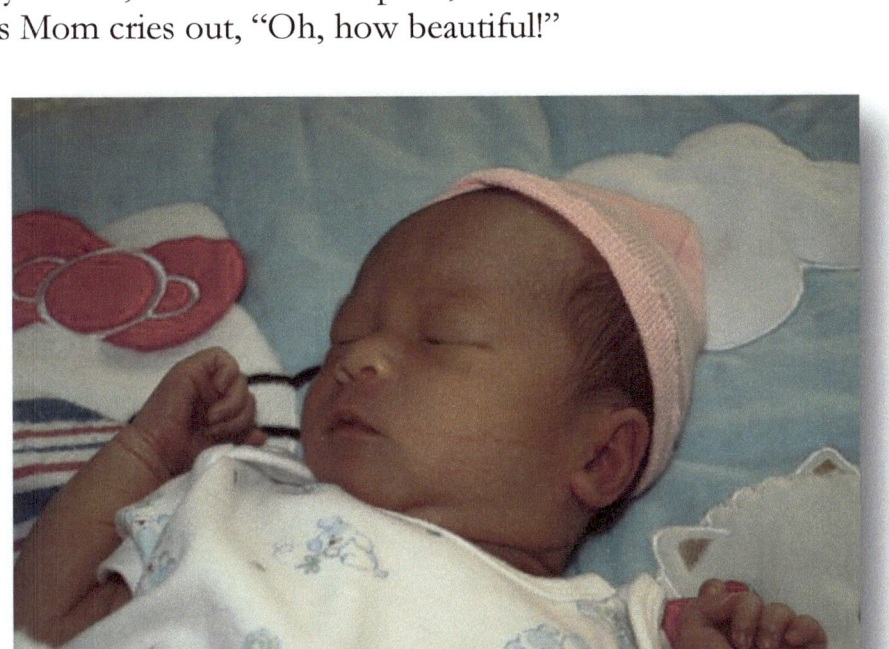

Clothes Make the Man

As a professional speaker, I take pride in my ability to have a good command of the English language and to choose exactly the right word for the proper occasion – to speak eloquently and to have people understand. But the stress of multiple speaking engagements, creating new programs, writing my

latest book, and managing a home and family had finally taken its toll. I knew I needed a release from the mounting pressures, and I decided to embark on a new and vigorous exercise program.

During the course of several months of working out at the local gym, I became acquainted with a nice older gentleman who always seemed in such high spirits. Both he and I looked like everyone else at the gym – hot, sweaty, and very unprofessional. But it was a time for exercise and improving our overall bodily health, so our appearance didn't concern us.

At a civic organization's monthly meeting, I happened to suddenly realize I was standing next to my older friend. Surprised to see him there, and in professional clothing, I heard myself say, "Mr. [Thompson], I didn't recognize you with clothes on!"

I couldn't believe it had come out of my mouth. I wanted the floor to open up and swallow me. I wanted a raging wind to sweep through the building and carry me away. I wanted to crawl under the nearest table—anything to escape!

However, I managed to regain my composure enough to say, "I am so used to seeing you in your work-out clothes at the gym." It was the best I could do on the spur of the moment, but I could hear the snickers … and see the raised eyebrows … and the shrugging shoulders. At least such recollections are useful for good anecdotal material!

MISCELLANEOUS

My Very Best Friend

He really is my very best friend –
has been now for many years.
He's sat beside me through many laughs,
But most importantly through many tears.

He has his opinion on various things –
Though he's often slow to express his thought.
He allows me to speak and often ramble
Before he reminds me of lessons he's often taught.

He knows what he likes and what he doesn't –
And he rarely changes his mind, if at all.
He seldom shares his own trials and hurts,
Yet listens to problems both great and small.

One could never ask for a better friend –
He's so genuine, there's nothing fake.
He's faithful and tender whatever the day,
That's my Beagle - my best friend Jake!

The Accident

I nearly killed my friend tonight –
My carelessness almost cost him his life.
It wasn't intentional, Heaven knows.
I'd never do that to my very best friend.

I've been up all night sitting by him –
Hearing him breathe and watching his chest.
I'm fearful each moment it will be his last.
And I'll blame myself if my friend truly dies.

I've asked his forgiveness so many times
During this long, lonely night as I sit by his bed.
I'm sure he'd forgive me if he could only speak.
But he lies there quiet, hopefully healing.

I'd left the chocolate on the bedroom floor
Where he found it and ate it—every bite!
Oh, please, my friend, dear Jake recover.
You know I love you—I'll be more careful!

And so I keep watch, my prayers go up.
I've cuddled him since he was a pup.
Morning comes, then two, then three,
With joy his full recovery I see!

Often some neglect that brings forth sadness
Brings forth a lesson received with gladness.
O, Lord, let me live more carefully –
There are so many who depend on me!

The Busy Brain

Oh, my brain, be quiet a spell –
Give me rest and a sense of quiet.
All folks want some "nothing" time
To simply sit and see the world.

Yet that isn't possible with the human brain,
For it was made to work and produce –
To keep us learning and going forward,
Not for sitting and vegetating.

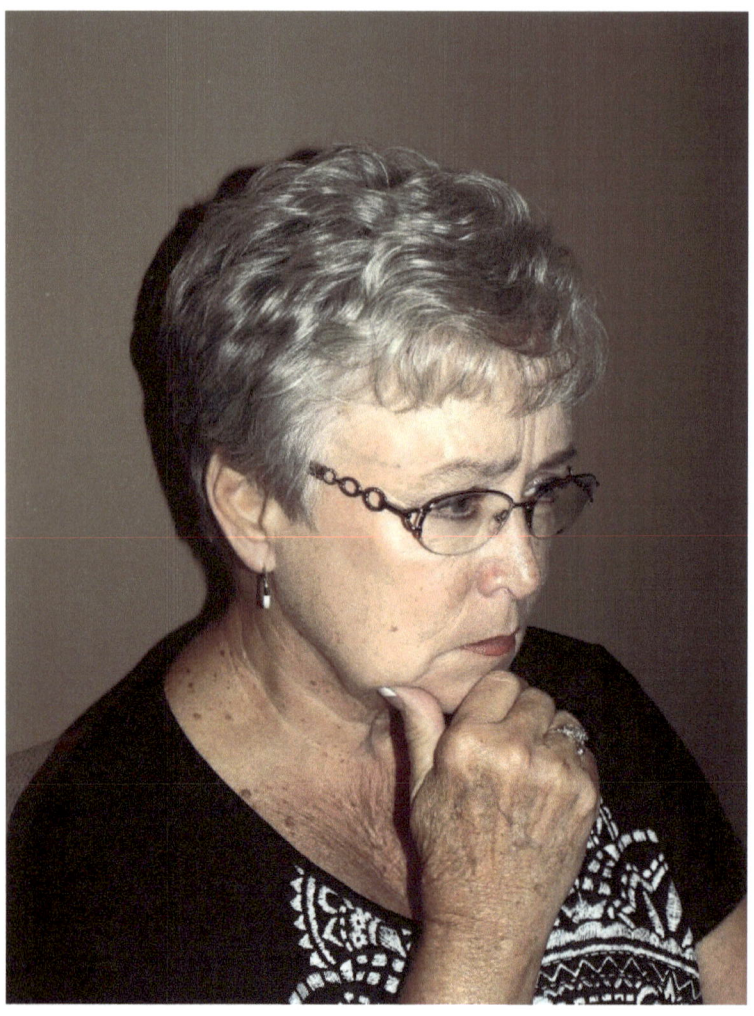

So when I ask my brain to simply "be,"
I am asking of it an impossible task.
For even in rest, it still absorbs –
Never stopping, never halting.

Thank you, brain, for working well,
For allowing me to see, hear and know
The wonders of God,
The wonders of ME!

This Empty House

I wander around in this empty house
With nothing to hear but the four fans' whirr.
The rooms have furniture, the halls have carpet,
But days crawl by in a cloudy blur.

The lamps are working, and the windows clean.
The ceilings are painted, the books are stacked
Things seem in order, and nothing's messy,
But the work around here I've recently slacked.

The house is quiet, the silence deafening,
And I often wonder what keeps me here.
The dog likes the yard, and I like the trees,
But the place is lacking of daily cheer.

I wish I were gone, just somewhere else.
The piano is silent, the organ just sits.
I enjoy the creek to some degree,
But I want my life back, not just pieces and bits.

But wait, I'm having a sudden thought
As I think through my thoughts and now realize –
This house isn't empty; I'm not alone.
The memories here are my valued prize.

The Clock on the Wall

It's nothing special, that clock on the wall. It has the ordinary shape of a circle (surrounded by a dull black outer casing), and its "face" is an uninspiring off-white. It must not be proficient in math, for it only counts to twelve. It never speaks except to sound an occasional alarm. That clock appears so unassuming and dull simply hanging there, and it has no qualities that would ordinarily command respect. Yet it frequently controls my life!

Clark (the name assigned to the clock) daily reminds me of the necessity of getting out of bed at a decent time. He states that lazy bodies produce lazy minds. Clark also tells me what time to go to bed at night, again reminding me that tired bodies produce tired minds. And as if that were not enough of his prescribed duties, he gives me the time for eating breakfast, telling me that if I do not get off to a good start, how do I expect to have a good day! And at lunch, he is quick to advise feeding my body the necessary nutrition. And, of course, at the dinner hour, Clark is quick to point out that my body can go only so long on that hopefully wholesome lunch I had.

On a more fun note, the clock on the wall reminds me that it's time for a refreshing time of afternoon relaxation with a good book, or a casual chat with a good friend. Or it may call out to me to notice that my poor, wonderfully friendly dog has spent much of the day lying alone in his bed and would relish my company for a few minutes of patting and his favorite treats. And on those special days, Clark calls out to me that it is time for my special genealogical, travel, or writing group meetings. Those meetings are such fun, and my good clock friend doesn't allow me to forego that opportunity.

It has been said that we are masters of our fate, yet I wonder if that clock is not the master of my fate as I daily watch those two little hands work their way around that circle, forever reminding me that IT may be the master of my fate.

An African friend of mine once said that there are no clocks in his village – that they go by the sun. Oh, what a nice release from that circular commander! But wait - without Clark, how would I know if it was 3:15 or 3:45? And how would I know when to eat, especially if my stomach were asleep and did not wake me up in time to prepare my food? Oh, Clark, perhaps you are not the commandeering dictator I first thought. You are, perhaps, my friend.

Quite a job, I'd say, for that ordinary-shaped round thing on the wall we call a clock!

The Invitation

As she entered the spacious Victorian-style home, it spoke of a close-knit family who enjoyed the finer things in life. Each family member had his or her own area of interest represented in the décor, yet there was a sense of flowing and unity in the variety it presented.

The furniture offered up a sense of comfort and ease, and it encouraged her to partake of their invitation to sit and share that evening of her life.

As she was ushered into the dining area, the table was set to perfection with the sterling silver flatware and cut crystal glassware, each reflecting the other's gleam. The fine linen tablecloth had been in the family for several generations although it still looked perfectly new. During a moment of silence, she thought she heard the cloth speak of many family dinners and memories it had had the privilege of enjoying. The linen napkins were folded precisely to accommodate their sterling silver holders.

The baked Alaskan salmon seasoned with lemon and pepper was done to perfection and served on the antique Petit Point patterned Haviland china. It was complimented by fresh asparagus in a simmering butter sauce, and the red-skinned potatoes offered up their own distinctive aroma of basil, oregano, and a hint of garlic.

The garden salad brought a sense of freshness that only a tenderly-cared-for family garden could produce. The spring mix of lettuce added to the colors of brilliant red radishes, yellow pepper, green cucumber, julienned orange carrots, and perfectly halved patio tomatoes. Such a succulent blend of anticipated flavors made it difficult for her to choose her desired dressing.

The finishing touch of three small scoops of lime, pineapple, and orange sherbet was presented in sterling dessert cups and served to cleanse her delighted pallet.

She accepted the invitation to the family's home, to their personal lives within the four walls, to a meal served with love that defied adequate description, and to an evening of unforgettable memories.
of unforgettable memories.

Hop Scotch House

The steep drive up the hill was a subtle, yet powerful, reminder that daily routines and responsibilities were about to be left behind and that the creative process would emerge in all of its beauty and energy in the hours and days to come. The asphalt was bumpy and one could not always see the smaller potholes. But it seemed to represent life – that change from one level of existence to another is often fraught with uneven paths and unseen difficulties. The circular drive that presented the house was also representative of the life cycle – that true existence is not a straight-lined, linear experience.

A worn, red brick sidewalk served as an invitation to what would become an extraordinary, creative process. The wooden ramp served as a wonderful reminder that those with disabilities can also contribute much to the arts and to society as a whole.

Two white columns on the front porch stood by quietly, yet they seemed to say, "I will support and encourage your efforts and sense of creativity while you stay within my protective structure. I will hold you up as you bring forth new literary life in the coming days."

The pointed porch roof punctuated the reality of high-rising hopes and dreams as it directed one's thoughts toward the bright blue sky with its white billowy clouds and cold wintry wind. The old door shouted, "Welcome" as it opened to the entrance of the home, making all who entered immediately feel they never wanted to leave this special place.

Upon entering the sunroom to the left, Mother Nature allowed herself to come inside through three glassed sides. She treated the visitor to giant swaying trees in the wind, the welcomed warmth of her sunshine, spacious fertile fields, and the escapades of scampering animals. Nature pleaded, "Soak in my endless beauty so that you, in turn, can pour it out again in various forms. Do not merely *look*. Truly *see* what I have in store for you. I will inspire you more than you can imagine".

The library to the right of the main entrance whispered, "Come in. Sit a while. Enjoy the warmth and glow of my fireplace, read, and plunge into the depths of my many books that you are free to browse through. Take time to

learn and appreciate your fellow artists and writers. Look at the tall trees standing outside my windows and remember that you, too, can stand firm during the winds of life. Learn that you must be flexible and bend, but you need not break during the storms you will encounter."

While the visitor was attempting to absorb the wisdom of the ages contained within the library, the larger living/dining area summoned. One felt both the protection of the three interior walls and the exposure of the southern-facing wall of sliding glass doors. The doors offered an invitation to step outside onto the adjacent patio and contemplate the rugged beauty of the rock garden and the vastness of the open fields. One heard the reminder that humans, too, need to be open to change and growth in order to survive.

A lone bird sat huddled in the crook of a leaf-bare tree as it trembled in the whistling wind. Was this poor feathered creature a victim of a malfunctioning navigational system, or did he simply prefer to spend the winter months in quiet solitude?

Deer leisurely strolled the fence line, comfortable in the presence of their nearby human visitors – secure, yet ever watchful, in their familiar surroundings. Their thin, frail-looking legs made one wonder how they could carry such large bodies as they bounded over fences, stone walls, and other obstacles in their paths. Yet those legs confirmed that size alone does not determine strength and ability.

The brilliant, round red berries in the dark green holly trees affirmingly reminded, "You see, there *can* be brightness in the midst of drabness."

The skyward-reaching trees stood naked in the winter chill and wind. But the trees reminded, "You do not have to be fancy and frilly to be happy and content. You need know only **who** you are, and **what** you are … to be what you were meant to be."

    In the southeastern corner of the northern pasture stood a monumentally-sized green ash tree, lovingly referred to as the "Keeper of the Meadow." The tree's large, upward-reaching limbs cried out, "Please, do not be afraid. I have stood guard over you these many decades, and I shall continue to do as long as I have life in my veins." The *Keeper* was marked with the scars of time, attesting to the fact that she, too, had suffered her share of hardships. Yet she stood gallantly and powerfully – daily a reminder to those around her of her faithfulness to her responsibility. She did not ask for praise and adoration. She merely asked to be noticed and appreciated. But regardless of whether or not she received the appreciation she desired, she would nonetheless continue to carry out her duties.

    The large, open kitchen invitingly called out, "Come and gather at my counter tops, and share your memories of family meals from the past. Sit at my table with your newly found friends and be encouraged to share your innermost thoughts. Allow your reflections to be the springboard of creativity to those around you. Enter into the spirit of camaraderie as you identify with others' stories. Be moved to respond to their concerns and hurts."

    The tiny storage room that was nestled behind the kitchen unobtrusively waited to share its supplies as needed. It made no demands and did not insist upon being heard. It quietly waited to be of service – always willing to give but realizing that it, also, needed to be restocked and refilled from time to time.

    The back door stood eloquently as both an entrance and an exit, allowing the house's occupants an alternative path in their desired destination – believing that options are good for the creative spirit.

The staircase leading to the second floor encouraged one to ascend to a higher level of existence and discovery. Each step offered additional encouragement and reminded one that the creative experience was truly a climb – but that with persistence, could be one step closer.

Each of the upper four bedrooms whispered, "Come. Stay with me and I will share with you the accumulated creative energy that is stored within my confines. This energy has been saved for you by those artists and writers who have come before you. They have left a legacy either upon which to build or to serve as an impetus to steer you into a new and perhaps uncharted direction."

Each room affirmed its support for the continuation of fertile imaginations as the fire of genius and talent was tended through ongoing observation and inspiration. Each room, while similar in structure and furniture content, offered its own unique treasure of discovery.

Two old barns teasingly encouraged exploration of themselves and their contents. Inside were long-ago-used horse stalls, and one could only imagine either the working, racing, or pleasure nature of the stalls' former inhabitants. One could almost hear the sound of swishing tails and nervous whinnies. The haylofts protected their treasures from the weather, and the old wooden ladders leading to them quietly encouraged an escapade to the lofts' higher levels. The worn rungs of the ladder attested to the fact that many trips had been made up and down those steps, and one could only imagine the reason for each trip. Had it been to carry up supplies? Had it been to check for unwanted varmints? Had it been to steal a few moments of quiet time away from the hustle and bustle of busy farm life? Or had it been to capture a precious experience with one's lover?

Pieces of farm equipment sat by quietly, almost unnoticed at first glance. Yet they spoke of readiness to perform whatever task necessary for the continuing productivity of the farm. Time had taken its toll on their appearance, for there was no longer shiny paint or sparkling metal. But their very presence attested to the fact that they were quite ready for efficient operation and that one's ability could not always be judged by outward appearances.

Next to the barns stood the naturalist's workshop. There was almost a sense of sacredness as one opened the door and saw "blessings from the land" inside. Broken gourds, sculptured by the elements of nature, hung from nails and sat upon various tables, waiting to be transformed into interior decorations. Gnarled honeysuckle vines and twigs were everywhere, some of which had been humanly woven into intricately-designed baskets. Twisted branches, seeds, pods, and sloughed-off snake skins served as a reminder that life come in many forms.

> This truly was a house and land upon which to gather – yet be alone,
> A place to do – yet think,
> A place to expand – yet draw into one's self,
> A place to pour out – yet fill up,
> A place to synthesize – yet analyze,
> A place to unite – yet separate,
> A treat externally – a healing internally,
> Other houses similar – yet none like this.

Those who retreated to this house and her ten acres were the shapers of fresh and unique handiwork in writing, painting, drawings, sculpture, dance, film-making, and the performing arts. They were the imaginative creators who bore artistic fruit. These individuals were able to retreat from the demands of their jobs, homes, and families for a brief period as they took time to nurture themselves and others who were staying with them during that nourishing time. Many of those who entered this house realized she was a living organism, giving back to her world as it had given to her.

> *Perhaps you would like to get away from the hustle and bustle of the world around you and travel to a quiet place where you can be alone with your thoughts— take in the serenity around you and breathe the fresh air. Let your mind wander and your body rest as you appreciate all your blessings. Take time to be thankful.*

IN MEMORY

A Young Man Named Derrick

He arrived on this earth in early summer
To the delight of his parents
Who had been waiting for him
Those long nine months.

He loved to fish and all those sports,
Also karate and R-O-T-C.
But his little dog he loved the most
As they shared that bond that none could break.

He dedicated his life to the things of God,
Took on His ways in his daily life.
His elders remarked he was a fine young man
Who made an impression wherever he went.

He was referred to as an All-American boy
Who daily displayed honesty and integrity.
He was never known to look for trouble,
But rather looked for those in need.

He took pride in his looks as young men do,
But also took pride in his fast-food job.
He was kind to those overlooked by others
And remembered his mother with a daily call.

He and his mother were especially close,
Though they sometimes argued
With their different views.
But their love was strong, continued to grow.

His life was cut short by an early death
That none saw coming and shocked everyone.
As his family grieved and wept hot tears,
He stood in the presence of Jesus above.

What does he teach us—this young man now gone?
To live each day, tomorrow may not be mine.
To reach out and love friends, family, and strangers –
For tomorrow may not give me the opportunity.

A Grandfather Named James

His name never appeared in the annals of history,
Nor was his name ever in bright, shining lights.
But to his grandson, he left a legacy far beyond price.
He is fondly remembered years after his death.
His impact on his life still has its effect.
He still lives on in John's mind and heart.

John called him "Granddad," this man he admired -
Who was born in 1881 in Garrard County, Kentucky.
He was a man of many talents – gardener and woodcarver
While he tilled the land as farmer, feeding his family,
Then made a stool from parts of a tree
Making the legs from limbs of that tree.

Granddad came from humble beginnings, starting his life in an old farmhouse
Where he learned to work hard as a very young boy,
And taught that work ethic to his own three sons –
Shirley, Bill, and John were the three boys' names.
While two little daughters, Lorene and Thelma,
Helped his wife in their little house.

Granddad even saved his grandson's life – not once, but twice,
    As young John, at eighteen months, fell into an old fish pond
And was rescued by his beloved Granddad.
    In later years, he saved John again in a personal way
        By being an example of manly good qualities.

This man was a man of not many words, but all knew him well
    For his actions spoke louder than numerous words.
The greatest impact Granddad had on young John
      Was the manner in which he treated Bertie - his wife.
        But John always knew her as Granny Lane.

Granddad loved little round Bertie, and everyone knew -
    Treat her well, or incur the wrath of her faithful James.
He showed his love for life-long mate by the look in his eyes
    And the sound of his voice.
        His special love – little Bertie Emily.

They married young, but their love held strong
    Through all the good times, even the bad.
They committed their lives, each to the other,
    And kept that commitment till the day they both passed.
        An example to family and friends alike.

The years wore on - the couple aged, their bodies grew old,
    But their love stayed strong, grew even stronger.
Granddad passed in 1966 – May 17th, his grandson's birthday.
    Such a sad day for grandson John –
        Yet knowing that Granddad had stepped into Heaven.

Bertie Emily – known to family as Granny –
    Lingered a few more years without her James
Until her death came in 1978, the 30th of October.
    But her family knows, they know full well
        They'll see them both again in Heaven.

Granddad worked various jobs during his many long years,
    From furniture sales to driving a truck for big Gulf Oil.
He didn't have a lot of "things" as the world often values,
    But everyone knew the man's moral stature.
        And that is a legacy beyond great price
            To leave to all, especially John.

Do you happen to have someone in your life who has been a positive influence to you over the years? If so, take a few moments to contact them and tell them how much they have meant to you. It will mean the world to them, especially if they are in their older years and reflecting back over their lives, wondering if they ever had an impact on anyone around them.

THE FIRST CHRISTMAS

It was her first Christmas without her mate,
And she wondered how she would do.
Her mind went back to the many before,
And the memories they shared in love.

She remembered the meals, the parties, the gifts
With warmth that surrounded her soul.
But things were different now, and he was gone
And the season she'd loved seemed hard.

Bob was kneeling now at the feet of his Lord,
Perhaps even singing in the Heavenly choir.
If there is Christmas in Heaven, she knew,
He'd be doing his part to ready the scene.

Yet knowing his joy and rejoicing for him,
Her heart was heavy and days seemed long.
But then Jesus spoke and her spirit lifted,
For He gave her a message she needed to hear.

"Remember, child, I am with you in Spirit and Truth,
Leading you, guiding you, loving you more.
Precious in My sight was the death of your mate,
You'll join him here when I call your name –
To live forever with all the saints.
The two of you will be joined again,
Never to be parted in My Heavenly realm."

Do you know someone who is experiencing
their first holiday season without their loved one?
If so, is there something you can do to help
them through those difficult days?

About the Author

Carol Goodman Heizer is a eight-time published author, speaker, and professional training and development leader whose books have sold both in the United States and overseas.

She holds a Bachelor of Arts degree in Drama and Public Speaking from Asbury College in Wilmore, Kentucky, and an M.Ed. degree in Secondary Education with concentration in English and Literature from the University of Louisville (Kentucky).

After teaching middle school and high school English and Writing for seventeen years, Carol opened Alpha Consulting and began speaking to various business, industrial, and educational groups. In addition, she conducted professional training and development seminars for clients such as the Department of Defense, Holiday Inn of America, Humana, the Louisville Board of Realtors, the Courier-Journal, General Electric, Purdue University, and Underwriters Safety and Claims.

Recognizing the need for her own personal and professional growth, Carol has been a Kentucky Speakers Association board member and an active member of National Speakers Association, Louisville Area Chapter of the American Society for Training and Development, Kentucky Society of Association Executives, and Ohio Christian Schools organization. She is also a member of Louisville Christian Writers and Kentucky Christian Writers.

Carol was columnist for several years for *Today's Woman* magazine, *International Clowning* newsletter, and the *Louisville, Kentucky, Chapter of Friendship Force International* newsletter.

She has hosted the local CNN affiliate WNAI radio station's call-in program titled *I've Been Thinking* that addressed local issues and featured individuals within the community who had a positive influence on their world.

Her writing has appeared on numerous occasions in *Chicken Soup for the Soul*.

Once asked how she ever kept up with her busy schedule, she replied, "I believe my life is a self-promoting cycle. What I am accomplishing brings me so much pleasure, it continues to give me more energy."

www.ingramcontent.com/pod-product-compliance
Lightning Source LLC
Chambersburg PA
CBHW042034150426
43201CB00002B/17